LIFE IS A GIFT
LOVE IS THE POINT

ADVANCE REVIEWS

"The tricky thing about a book like this one from Ryan is that it's words on a page, because obviously all books are words on pages—and Ryan is a wonderful writer and his voice hums on these pages, so all good there—but oh my god, this book is about a man dying and being reborn over and over again, not because something went wrong, but because he just keeps saying yes to being Ryan; and that kind of life—the kind that wrecks you as it resurrects you, as it breaks you open in a vast communion with the ones you love and all of creation around you—writing about that, trying to communicate what it's like to be caught up in that, capturing the fullness of that on white pages with black letters is nearly impossible, and yet this fella comes astonishingly close because as I went along on the ride with Ryan as he kept finding his way into even greater Ryanness, I found myself thrilled and moved and inspired to be me in new ways, and I can't imagine higher praise for a book."

—Rob Bell, author, speaker, playwright, and musician

"Ryan Meeks is a man of rare courage. Life has taken him for a ride requiring nothing less than the complete transformation of ego into a heart-centred life. This is an elegantly written biography describing a journey from epistemological certainty to unknowing, from public adulation to suffering the solitude of the prophet, from belief-based religion to trusting personal experience, from allegiance to a false God to inhabiting the Great Mystery which is the fate of every true mystic. There is life-changing wisdom found in these pages, gained through authentic suffering, the facing of fears, broken-heartedness, but above all, an unswerving commitment to allowing love to have its way."

—Bruce Sanguin, psychotherapist, author, and speaker

"Written with poetic poignancy, herein lies a humble, truthful, wise story born through suffering and courage that will surely inspire you to live true and free. If you have outgrown your religious belief system or your constrictive worldview or both, this book is especially for you."

—Phileena Nikole, author of *Mindful Silence* and *Pilgrimage of a Soul*

"I love this book! It's a story of how a person's religion of certainty can die and be buried and then, to his own surprise, a beautiful and honest spirituality can arise from its ashes. But to me, it's even more: it's a real story of a real person I know and have watched go through this agonizing but beautiful process. Joyfully recommended!"

—Brian D. McLaren, author, speaker, activist, and public theologian

"This book is a rare wellspring of honesty, exploration, and insight. Few people can tell their story without being preachy, but Ryan does so with humor and grace. Real spiritual and psychological change is rare these days, and here is a firsthand account. It's not a book that will tell you what to do, but Ryan's story of courage and love is full of hidden pathways and possibilities for those of us seeking a more authentic and rich spiritual life. 'Life is gift, love is the point' is not some cliché. It's born from real pain, grace, and truth. Read this book instead of scrolling."

—Kent Dobson, author, wilderness guide, and pastor

LIFE IS A GIFT LOVE IS THE POINT

HOW I LOST MY FAITH, KILLED MY CHURCH, SAVED MY LIFE, AND FOUND MY SOUL

RYAN MEEKS

*grafo*house

TULSA | GUADALAJARA

Life Is a Gift. Love Is the Point.
© 2025 by Ryan Meeks

Published by Grafo House Publishing
Tulsa, Oklahoma | Guadalajara, Mexico

ISBN 978-1-963127-45-4 (paperback)
978-1-963127-46-1 (ebook)

Cover design by Edgar Pulido

Printed in the United States of America

28 27 26 25   1 2 3 4

To the God I don't believe in anymore—
Thank you for the language that carried me until it couldn't.
For the fire I mistook for certainty.
For the ache I once called longing.
You were never what I thought,
but maybe you were listening anyway.
Or maybe just the idea of you
was enough to keep me searching for what's real.
And in that way,
you did not fail me.

"In the middle of the journey of our life I came to myself within a dark wood where the straight way was lost."
—Dante Alighieri

"Everything I've ever let go of has claw marks on it."
—Anne Lamott

CONTENTS

PART I
MAKING AND BREAKING

CHAPTER 1
THANK GOD

"If we cannot tell a story about what happened to us,
nothing has happened to us."
—James P. Carse

Cancer?! Oh, thank God.

I didn't say that out loud. That would've freaked everyone out. But inside, something gave up. Like I'd been holding my breath for years and finally got to exhale.

I can still go right back to that moment. The room smelled like disinfectant and burnt coffee. I heard the click of a pen, the hum of the lights; I felt a rising numb sensation in my hands. Relief and dread crashed together, impossible to tell apart.

Immediately my mind started cycling through mental frameworks, trying to build meaning out of chaos.

This is the death descent Jung talks about.
This is evolutionary pruning.
This is my body absorbing the stress of the last few years.

I didn't believe the old theology anymore, but interpretation had always been my way of staying in control. If I could name it, I could manage it. If I could turn it into a concept, I wouldn't have to feel it.

But underneath the noise in my head was the truth I didn't want to admit: something in me was glad to be sick. Elated, really.

Finally, there was a reason to stop—a reason no one could argue with or blame me for. For the first time in forever I didn't have to keep going.

Because by the time I got the diagnosis in 2017, I was already collapsing on the inside.

I'd spent years deconstructing the theology I once preached, publicly shifting my views, interrogating scripture, advocating for LGBTQ+ inclusion—and watching my church hemorrhage in the process. We went from *Time* magazine calling us a model of modern faith to consolidating our eight campuses into one after losing two-thirds of our community.

I was still preaching, still leading, still trying to offer something real. But the cost was mounting. Every Sunday felt like another round in a theological cage match—me versus the Bible, versus tradition, versus the version of God I had lost touch with. Some people stayed, bless them. Some people left loudly, while others left quietly, with long emails that began with "I love you, but…"

I didn't blame them. I was changing fast. Too fast for some, not fast enough for others. I was letting go of the beliefs I had been handed as absolute truth, but I hadn't landed anywhere solid yet.

I wasn't a pastor who *had been* on a journey. I was *on* one. In real time. Falling apart and waking up, all at once.

Still, I kept going. For my staff. For my family. For the dream I had spent my whole adult life building. For the story that had shaped me, even as it failed me.

But I was tired.
Bone tired.
Soul tired.

The week before my diagnosis, I was in a Raja Yoga class at Ananda Temple in Bothell, Washington. That week's mantra was: "I accept whatever comes my way as an opportunity for growth."

Then I got the results from the biopsy…

Lymphoma.

I remember thinking, *Well, that's cute.* My life already felt like a three-ring circus on fire—with a dramatically thinned-out audience—but sure, bring it.

Funny enough, I didn't feel fear. Not yet. Just…stillness.

Cancer didn't end my world. It gave me permission to stop spinning it.

No more sermons. No more meetings. No more theological debates in the church lobby. Just silence. And breath. And doctors and scans and naps and waiting rooms. And the space to finally tell the truth—not to everyone else, but to myself. The relief felt foreign, almost guilty—like I'd snuck out of my own life.

The truth was: I didn't want to rebuild.
Not the church.
Not the brand.
Not the belief system.

I didn't want to fight to save something that had already died. At some point, you have to let go of the life you thought you were building and say yes to the one that's actually trying to happen. I wanted to rest. I wanted to be human again.

That's what cancer gave me. Not clarity. Not a new theology. *Space.* Space to let all the pieces fall and see what still had heat.

And something did.

It wasn't faith, exactly, at least not the kind I used to preach. But something simpler. More embodied. I started noticing what was still alive in me. Still trustworthy. Still true.

My kids. My wife. My breath.
The taste of food.
The sun on my neck.
The deep sense that life, even now, was mysteriously, undeservedly good.

I started wondering if that was enough. If maybe God wasn't found in belief or belonging or performance, but in the raw gift of being. In *this*—whatever *this* was.

And eventually, words began to form. A simple mantra that started whispering its way through me:

Life is a gift.
Love is the point.

That pair of sentences centered me. It gave me a place to stand. And it's been enough to build a new life on after losing it all.

This isn't a story about cancer. It's not even a story about losing faith or killing my church, although we'll talk about those things.

It's about shedding old gods. About releasing the grip of certainty. About what happens when your entire worldview collapses, and some-how—*somehow*—you're still here. Still breathing. Still capable of joy. Still able to love.

It's about saving your life and finding your soul.

It's also about learning to trust life again. Not because it's fair or easy or controllable. But because it's *real*. And it's enough.

If you've ever felt the floor drop out, the center give way, the story stop working…I wrote this for you.

You're not lost.
You're not broken.
You're just in it.

The real stuff. The disorienting, beautiful, no-map terrain of being alive.

And yeah, it can be confusing.
It can wreck you.
But it can also free you.

To be honest, I put this book off for years. Friends kept asking when I'd write it all down—the church, the collapse, the cancer, whatever came after. I kept dodging. Partly because life was unfolding faster than I could type. Partly because I wasn't sure the world needed another deconstruction memoir. And mostly because I knew I'd probably argue with myself in three years—so why put anything in ink?

Also, writing about this stuff still felt too raw. Like trying to explain something that was still happening in me. I needed to put a few more miles under me before circling back.

Back when I was still a pastor, a couple of Christian publishers reached out. "We'd love to publish your first book," they said. They wanted the tidy version of me. Neat theology. Linear success. Sermon-series-turned-chapters. A feel-good faith journey with just enough drama to keep the small group discussion spicy.

But all I could hear was that David Bazan lyric:

> Another young man tells his story
> before his heart has even broken one time.

That was me.
Earnest. Unscarred. Cosplaying certainty.
So I passed on their offers.

Time, loss, and chemo took care of the heartbreak quota. Whatever else this book is, at least it's not being written ahead of the pain. If the pages feel a little scarred, a little scratched up—good. They should.

I should also point out that this book isn't a defense, a theological argument, or a clever subtweet to win back anyone who left. Honestly, nothing in here is going to change the minds of my critics. If anything, I'm sure I've included enough to confirm their worst suspicions.

I used to tell our church that if people criticized what we were doing, they could just respond, "It's worse than you think."

I'm certain this book will make that clear.

But for others—maybe for you—this might arrive like a healing salve. A confirmation that you're not crazy. You're not alone. And there might just be light at the end of the tunnel.

Like our old slogan at EastLake, I hope this book serves in some way to be *a beneficial presence in the world, and a pain in the ass to fear-based religion.*

A few caveats. First, I'm not offering a new system. Especially not one built on certainty. This is a compass, not a cage. A story, not a script. You're still going to have to find your own way.

Second, it's a work in progress. The conclusions are provisional. If you ask me next year, I'll probably say things differently or regret a few of these reflections. Likely.

And third, it's an invitation. If something resonates, follow it. If not, move past it. Ultimately, this isn't "the way." It's just how it went down and where I find myself now as a result.

I don't know if there's one clean throughline to all of this. But I've started to notice something in the process of writing:
Part of this book is simply an attempt to be seen.
Not as a hero. Not as a heretic. But as a human

For a long time, I lived in extremes, projected onto as a Christlike leader or a dangerous apostate.
I was a mega-church messiah or Satan incarnate.
I was either saving souls or deceiving them.
There wasn't much room in the middle.

Somewhere in that tension, and somewhere in these pages, you can find the real me. And, I hope, you'll find the real you.

I hope this book makes you laugh a little. Maybe even cry. I hope you see pieces of your own journey in these pages. And I hope you find the quiet confidence to trust the transformation of your own human life.

Because after all, this life truly is a gift.

That conviction keeps evolving, but it still feels like the truest thing I know.

CHAPTER 2
CHURCH KID

"You can kiss your family and friends good-bye
and put miles between you,
but at the same time you carry them with you...
because you do not just live in a world but a world lives in you."
—Frederick Buechner

I grew up in church. Like, *in* it.

I spent more time in the sanctuary than in my living room. It wasn't just Sunday mornings—it was Sunday nights, Wednesday small group, Saturday set-up, potlucks, Bible studies, lock-ins, worship nights.

If the doors were open, we were there.
And honestly, I loved it.

The smell of the carpet. The sound of plastic chairs dragging on linoleum. The warmth of the people who called me by name. The way the pastors knelt down to talk to me like I mattered. And Jim—an older guy who always had Tic Tacs in his pocket—would pop the lid open with a grin and hand me a few, like a tiny communion between us.

I loved going in early with my dad on Sundays. He was a pastor, and I got to ride shotgun as he sang worship songs with one hand lifted to heaven then spritzed Binaca before we went inside—breath sanctified. I'd walk in behind him like I had backstage access to God. And in a way, I did.

Because this was more than ritual or religion for me.
It was home.
It was purpose.
It was magic.

My church wasn't small. By the time I was in elementary school, it was one of the largest charismatic churches in the Seattle area. It was the early eighties, and we were part of the post-Jesus Movement wave—Pentecostal, passionate, prophetic.

We raised our hands. We prayed for the sick. We believed God could speak directly to us. And we wanted more of it. More fire. More power. More Jesus.

I would stay there all day every Sunday, sitting through multiple services, helping staff and volunteers, handing out bulletins, greeting people, stacking chairs. I felt seen. I felt important. I felt like I belonged to something that mattered.
And I did.

By the time I hit junior high, I couldn't wait to get into youth group.

This was the era of fog machines, bad drama skits, emotional altar calls, and an endless parade of youth pastors who all seemed to be recovering from something. It was a little chaotic. A little ridiculous.

We sang songs about being warriors for God. We wept at retreats and rededicated our lives every time someone told a testimony that ended in jail or addiction recovery. We watched videos about the rapture. We considered throwing out all our secular CDs—and then didn't. We made lists of unsaved friends to "reach" for Jesus. Youth group was part revival, part pep rally, part spiritual boot camp.

I wasn't dragged to church—I dragged other people there. I was the kid who rallied the squad. I brought my public school friends. I hosted sleepovers so I could bring them to youth group in the morning. I was equal parts mischievous and devout, and somehow that combo worked for me.

I believed in the mission. I believed God was using me. And I believed we had the answers to what everyone needed most.

I remember one night during my seventh-grade year, one of the pastors pulled me aside after a service. He looked me in the eye with this quiet seriousness, like he was about to share a secret from God himself.

He told me he saw leadership in me. He said that God had His hand on my life and that I had a calling.

Then he prophesied over me, right there, and he said I'd be a vital part of God's work in the world. People would follow my lead. I would speak and others would hear the voice of the Spirit.

And I believed him. Because, deep down, I already felt it. I carried this invisible sense of urgency. Like my life was supposed to mean something, and I had to connect with it.

That moment gave language and confirmation to the inner current I didn't know how to name.
It felt like a spiritual initiation.
It felt sacred.
It felt like my yes.

And from that point on, I started shaping myself around it. Around being someone God could use.

But even before that, the first hints of doubt and inadequacy had already started to surface.

I don't think I understood the difference between *wanting* to believe and actually *believing*. I knew I didn't feel the same things everyone around me seemed to be claiming—these intense, dramatic spiritual experiences—but I was certain I wanted to. And I assumed that wanting it badly enough, and trusting it *could* be true, had to count as faith.

So I stayed close. I sang the songs. I cried at the altar.
And I hoped that eventually,
the inside would catch up with the outside.

When puberty hit, something began to shift.
That's when the sweetness of faith got tangled up with pressure.
That's when belonging started to depend on purity.

Suddenly the sermons were about sex. Lust. Modesty. Guarding your heart.

We were told that our bodies were sacred temples—but also kind of gross and dangerous. That sex was beautiful, but only in marriage. And even then, we should probably keep the lights off and play Christian music in the background.

I was a teenager with hormones, a good heart, and zero tools to understand what was happening in my body. I begged God to fix me. To make me pure. To make me holy. To make me not want what I wanted. But the harder I tried, the more tangled my heart became.

And I wasn't alone. Everyone around me seemed to be repenting for the same things: impure thoughts, lustful eyes, crossing invisible lines with their boyfriend or girlfriend, masturbating and then pledging never to do it again.

It was like we were all gasping for air inside a purity-themed escape room.

At some point in this hormonal hurricane, I discovered Christian death metal.

Bands like Vengeance Rising and Mortification became my sanctuary. The music was aggressive, weird, loud as hell—and explicitly Christian. It was the one place where I could feel all the rage and confusion and energy of adolescence without getting judged for it.

These guys weren't trying to be sensitive to spiritual seekers.
They weren't ashamed of the headline.
They screamed about hell.
They named demons.
They said what most preachers in my life were only implying:
You're probably going to burn in hell unless you get it together.

The violence of the cross, the horrors of hell—it was both a warning and a promise. These bands were unapologetically open about it, carrying the message in distorted guitars and guttural screams. And I was drinking it in, thirsting for truth, even if that truth was terrifying. (To get an idea, go listen to the end of "Beheaded" by Vengeance Rising or the beginning of "Slay the Wicked" by Deliverance.)

The message was clear: God's righteous thirst could only be slaked by the blood of Jesus—a gruesome, relentless hunger satisfied through cosmic violence. Ironically, a perfect album cover for Slayer. That image stuck with me, lodged deep in my imagination, mixing awe and disgust in a way no preacher's sermon ever did.

I should've been horrified. But I wasn't.
I felt the honesty.

Because that was the theology already forming inside me.

That bad news always accompanies good news.

That God is love, but also kind of furious.

That sin is so severe it required a magical bloody murder to be forgiven.

That my body would sabotage my soul if I slipped for even a second.

It's wild to look back now and realize that the love I thought was forming me was also planting seeds of fear.

But that's how it works, isn't it? When you're young, you don't separate the sweetness from the fear or the shame. It's all one story. One system. One God.

Looking back, I can see how much that era gave me.

It gave me community.

It gave me structure.

It gave me adults who paid attention to me.

It gave me language for purpose.

It gave me a stage to grow on.

It gave me a story that helped make sense of life.

But it also gave me scripts I didn't know how to unlearn. And to be fair, not all those scripts were bad. Rules can hold us when they're rooted in love. But when they're built on fear, they start to shape-shift into shame.

They taught me that my worth was tied to obedience.

That doubt was a slippery slope.

That desire was a liability.

That questions were dangerous.

That silence meant God was testing me.

And it laid the groundwork for a fracture that would take decades to notice.

What held me wasn't just belief. It was beauty. It was music. It was community. It was the sincere hope that love was real and life was good.

And I'm not here to throw that away.
But I am here to tell the truth.
That the story I was given—however well-intentioned—also taught me to split myself in two.

CHAPTER 3
A GOSPEL OF
DISCONNECTION

"You do not have to be good.
You do not have to walk on your knees
for a hundred miles through the desert, repenting."
—Mary Oliver, Wild Geese

Before I ever held a mic or led a prayer, I was already gone. Gone from my body, from my instincts, from the inner voice that whispered, "This doesn't feel right."

I grew up in a world where spiritual maturity meant distrusting yourself.
Where we were told to "lean not on our own understanding."
Where holiness meant suppression.
Where human desire wasn't something to be honored or explored—it was a threat. A test. A trap.

We were discipled into shame before we understood our own biology. The body was suspect. The heart was deceitful. Desire was a slippery slope that ended in hell. And sexuality was a fire we were meant to fear and never touch.

We didn't get sex education.
We got temptation awareness.

We were warned about "stumbling blocks," which mostly meant women's bodies. We were taught to bounce our eyes, pray away our urges, and imagine our future wife every time we masturbated. Which, technically, we weren't supposed to do—but I remember a few more realistic small group volunteers who offered this as a consolation prize, a life hack for the inevitable.

At youth camp one summer, there was a whole chapel night devoted to the sin of lust. All day long, the talk in our cabin was about boobs. This girl's boobs, that girl's boobs, a fiery debate over Pamela Anderson's versus Cindy Crawford's. Someone made a joke about Jeremy's mom's boobs, which derailed things in an awkwardly vivid direction. We talked about girls. We talked to girls. We watched them play volleyball like our souls depended on it. It wasn't subtle. Hormones were running the show.

And then came chapel.

The lights dimmed. The worship band cued up a breathy set of emotionally sensual songs, inviting us to ask God to "touch us deeply in the secret place."

No one blinked at the phrasing. No one thought it odd that we went straight from fantasizing about girls to crying out for divine intimacy.

We just…switched altars. Same hunger, different music.

We didn't know how to process anything we were feeling.
We didn't have the words.
We didn't have permission.

We just had this unspoken understanding that whatever we were experiencing was wrong—but also normal—but also bad—but also inevitable—but also…?

After worship came the sermon.
Fire and guilt.

We were told what lust does to the soul. What it does to women. What it does to God. Then came the altar call. And like always, half the room went forward, crying, rededicating themselves to Jesus, repenting for kissing someone, or touching themselves, or having thoughts they couldn't stop.

And like always, the other half of the room said they had "unspoken" prayer requests. We all knew what that meant. "Unspokens" were always something sexual. Something dark and secret and vaguely deviant.

Which, of course, made them fascinating.

In a weird way, the shame made it hotter. The very thing we weren't allowed to name became the gravitational center of the entire group.

We weren't being purified.
We were being sexualized by our own repression.
And we didn't know how to talk about it.

Looking back, we didn't need better rules.
We needed language.
We needed safety.
We needed to know that being human wasn't the same thing as being sinful.

But instead, we learned to split in two. We learned to confuse disconnection with devotion, to spiritualize shame, to mistrust our bodies, our longings, and our instincts.

Here's the craziest part: I was already in love.

Michelle and I were teenagers, but what we had was real. We were writing letters. Flying back and forth from Seattle to San Diego. Dreaming of a future.

And we were also having sex.
Not casually. Not recklessly.
Lovingly. Passionately. Sometimes awkwardly. Always intensely.
And it was beautiful.

But every time we gave ourselves to each other physically, the shame came roaring back. We'd cry. Repent. Pledge to start over. Swear to save ourselves for the wedding night even though we both knew we wouldn't.

It was confusing, sacred, electric, guilt-ridden, and transcendent all at the same time. And I wouldn't have said it this way back then, but being inside her, holding her, melting into each other—that was the closest I had ever felt to God.

And still, I believed it was a sin.

Because everything in my formation told me the sacred couldn't live in the skin.
That real love was something you had to protect by waiting.
That sexual desire and divinity couldn't share the same breath.

So I kept fracturing. Kept disembodying myself. Kept rejecting my humanity in the name of spirituality because I was told they couldn't co-exist outside a very narrow framework of rules and circumstances.

I thought God demanded my disconnection.
Was it really temptation, or was I just resisting my own incarnation?

CHAPTER 4
WHAT HELD ME

"Transcend and include.
Go beyond—but never forget what brought you here."
— Ken Wilber

For all the damage, there were gifts. For all the shame, there was beauty. For all the certainty that collapsed, there were moments that still shimmer.

Before I say more about what I no longer believe, I want to pause and name what was good. What held me.

I was held by music.
Not just the lyrics, but the way a room full of people would lift their voices in unison. I've seen people cry who hadn't cried in years because the chords swelled at the right moment and they felt safe enough to let go.

Some of those worship songs still live in my bones. They carried something honest when I needed it. Longing. Reverence. Hope. Beauty. Sometimes I hum one without noticing, a phantom limb of old beliefs.

And those songs did what scripture often couldn't:
They softened me.
They let me feel.

I was held by community.

By potlucks and hospital visits and prayer circles. By grandpas with Tic Tacs and moms with casseroles and friends who knew the sound of your voice when you muttered a fake "I'm fine."

The church wasn't always a place of judgment for me.
For long stretches, it was a place of compassion.

I was surrounded by people trying to love well in the best ways they knew how. People who showed up to celebrate, and grieve, and hold your kid when you needed two free hands. People who didn't need a reason to care about you.
And that mattered.

I was held by structure.

By rhythm. By ritual.
By the grounding power of returning to something.

Church gave me a reason to pause each week. A reason to confess, to sing, to reflect, to belong.

Although I don't identify with that system any longer, there are times I still feel the ache for sacred rhythm. To be part of something bigger and safer and more certain than me, something that reminds me it matters to keep going.

I was held by language.

By the idea that we were meant to serve the least of these.
That love is patient.
That justice rolls down like a mighty river.
That faith without works is dead.

24

That we are all one

I don't quote the Bible like I used to.
But I still carry those phrases around in my pocket.
They shape how I see the world.
They still speak.

I was held by my parents.
They never focused on doctrine when I was growing up. I honestly don't remember a single theological debate in our house as a kid. What I do remember is how much their faith looked like gratitude, love, and service.

Even though they held conservative views—around behavior, around sexuality—what they lived out was something softer, more open-hearted. The Christianity I saw in them wasn't about control or fear. It was about caring for people.

It was a faith that proclaimed, by word and by action, that everyone is included, no matter who they are or what they've done.

Later, as an adult, we'd discuss theology more directly.
But the foundation had already been laid.
Not the beliefs, but the tone. The love. The wide welcome.
That held me.

I was held by longing.
Even at its worst, my faith was trying to reach something good.
Even when it missed the mark, it was chasing love.

And while I don't believe what I used to believe about God,
I still believe in the thing that made me reach in the first place.

That ache to be part of something beautiful.
To touch something transcendent.
To live with integrity.
To give more than I take.
To follow what is good, and true, and whole.

Philosopher Loyal Rue once said that religion, at its best, helps us remember the past with gratitude instead of regret, anticipate the future with hope instead of despair, and inhabit the present with a sense of inspired responsibility in community.
That rings true.
I've seen it, and I've lived it.

For many years, religion shaped how I made sense of the world. It gave me a story to live inside. A reason to get up in the morning. A way to name the ache and awe of being alive. I had community and purpose. I had language for love and mystery.

For all its flaws, religion can offer people a lifeline when nothing else makes sense.

I know my childhood was dramatically better because my parents were Christians. Especially when it comes to my dad. My mom had a loving family, but my dad came from almost nothing—poverty, instability, a home that didn't teach safety or tenderness.

Finding Jesus as a teenager gave him something to hold onto. It gave him a playbook he wasn't given anywhere else. His faith helped him become the kind of father he never had. It raised him up and taught him how to be a better dad and a better human. I got to grow inside the stability he learned from being discipled by solid, kind Christian men.

So much of the head start I had in life—structure, community, a sense of purpose—came from the virtues my parents learned in church. I may not share the beliefs anymore, but I'll never stop being grateful for the love that reached my family through that door.

That's why I think it's short-sighted—sometimes even arrogant—when people say they hope organized religion disappears altogether. I understand the impulse. I've felt it too. But if every person who still depends on religion suddenly lost their belief overnight, it wouldn't usher in some enlightened utopia. It would cause a massive rupture—personally, socially, and culturally.

Religion still provides coherence and stability for billions. For morality. For belonging. For knowing where you stand in the world and how to be of service to others. It's more than a belief system. It's a container.

And we're already seeing what happens when that container collapses without something equally meaningful to replace it.

The rise of the "nones"—those who check "none" when asked their religious affiliation—is one of the most significant spiritual shifts of our time. But along with that exodus comes a quiet epidemic of loneliness, fragmentation, and disconnection.

People may have escaped toxic theology or institutional control, but many no longer know how to locate themselves in a larger story. They don't know where to bring their grief, their awe, or their longing to help. They don't know how to belong to something sacred together.

It's not enough to walk away.
We have to decide what we're walking toward.

Growth is slow. People don't leap from one worldview to another in a single breath. Every stage of meaning-making has its own purpose, and for many, religion still offers the kind of soil where something essential can grow.

I needed that once. And I'm grateful I had it.

I didn't leave religion because I was better or braver than those who stay. I left because I had to keep going. I'm still finding out what that means, but I can look back with real gratitude.

The well I drank from once gave me life.
And I wouldn't be here without it.

CHAPTER 5
THE GOD WHO WOULDN'T SPEAK

"The most common sort of lie
is that by which a man deceives himself."
—Nietzsche

Growing up, I wanted God to speak to me.
Like, *actually* speak to me.

I grew up around people who said he did. Constantly. God told them
who to marry. What house to buy. What to say to a stranger at Safeway.
My friends wept at the altar after youth group because they "felt the
presence of the Holy Spirit," and I wept too—but more often because
I didn't feel anything at all.

I tried. God knows I tried. I lifted my hands during worship. I repented
for every possible sin I could think of, even things I wasn't sure were
sins. I fasted. I begged. I lay awake at night whispering prayers and
waiting for some sign, some flicker in my chest that meant he saw me.

Nothing. Except the growing sense that I was the problem.

What if my heart wasn't right?
What if I wasn't desperate enough?
What if there was some secret sin buried deep—an invisible soul
tumor keeping God away?

Because *everyone else* seemed to be getting it. Speaking in tongues. Hearing prophetic words for other people. Feeling God's love like a physical sensation. Meanwhile I was still trying to figure out if the goosebumps during worship were spiritual or just a result of the sub-zero AC in the sanctuary. Every rare mountaintop moment was tangled with the doubt that I was just making it all up.

Looking back now, I think it was the story of being chosen that kept me in.

Not in a grand, destiny sense. Just...noticed. Known. Confirmed. I didn't need a burning bush. I would've settled for a warm feeling in my gut. Anything to assure me that God wasn't only an idea I inherited but a Presence I could actually experience.

But the silence stretched on.

And in that silence, I tried to be faithful. I remembered the story of Doubting Thomas and how Jesus said, "Blessed are those who haven't seen and yet believe." That lodged in me somewhere deep. What if that was the shape my faith was meant to take? Quiet, steady, devoted?

I started telling myself that the silence *was* the point. My calling wasn't to hear voices or see visions—it was to trust anyway. To obey. To follow. To live a life of surrendered consistency.

Maybe I was called to serve from the valley. Maybe the ache itself was my offering.

So I kept showing up. I kept trusting. I chose to believe—not because I saw, but precisely because I didn't.

I wanted to be near to God, but I had confused belonging to a group with nearness to God. I belonged to a spiritual community. I belonged to a faith tradition. But I wasn't close to anything real. At least not in the way I was taught to expect. I had learned to mimic nearness.

Raise your hands here. Say amen there. Push through the dryness. God is testing you. God is building your faith. God is always speaking—are you listening?

Yes, I was listening.
And no—I didn't hear a thing.

But I couldn't say that out loud. Not then.

So I said the next best thing: nothing.

And for years, the silence between me and God echoed louder than any song I sang or sermon I heard preached.

CHAPTER 6
MY FANTASTIC RIDE
DOWN THE SLIPPERY SLOPE

"There lives more faith in honest doubt, believe me,

than in half the creeds."

—Alfred Tennyson

Michelle and I got married in 1998 in a church with a pipe organ, Bibles stacked in pews, and my dad officiating. There were flowers, rings, and a room full of people—many who loved us, and probably more than a few who thought we were way too young and completely out of our minds. Also, sorry to everyone who showed up hoping for an open bar. We were underage.

A few years later, in 2004, we started a church. I was 25 years old. A handful of friends, some garbage sound gear, and a junior high cafeteria we rented on Sunday mornings. We would show up at 6 a.m. to unload the truck, set up chairs, rig the projectors, plug in the microphones, and set up the kids' rooms. I'd lead the music team, then wipe my forehead, grab a mic, and walk back up to preach. Afterward, I'd meet and greet all the folks who attended, then tear it all down and load up the truck again.

It was exhausting. And we loved it.

We weren't trying to build a megachurch. We were just trying to build a church we wouldn't be embarrassed to invite our friends to. Something real. Something honest. We wanted to create a place where we could talk about God without all the nitpicking religious extras. A place for people who had honest questions and still wanted to belong.

And somehow it worked. Fast.

We grew to thousands of people in just a few years. We added campuses. Built a staff. Upgraded the equipment. We became one of *those* stories. A church planting success. We got invited to speak at conferences. We were featured in magazines.

Some weeks, there'd be white rental vans in the parking lot—church staff teams from across the country who'd flown in to observe a weekend, hoping to take home best practices. I consulted with pastors, spoke at national events, even helped film a Bible study curriculum that went out to tens of thousands of churches around the world.

It was surreal. Humbling. A little absurd.
And exhilarating.

But once I wasn't loading chairs or leading worship or driving the gear truck anymore—once I finally had a staff and a rhythm and time to breathe midweek—something happened. Something as unsettling as it was unexpected.

I slowed down enough to hear myself think.

There's a certain mercy in being too busy to unravel. When I was driving the truck, setting up the chairs, leading the music, preaching the sermon, then tearing it all down. I was moving too fast and preaching too loudly to hear the slow cracking sound in my chest.

But now I had a team, systems, and infrastructure. I wasn't scrambling to build anymore. And with that came silence.

The thoughts that filled this newfound silence weren't new. They were dusty and familiar. Things I'd shelved years earlier during youth group, or in my Old Testament class at Bible college when I asked one too many questions and got labeled "disruptive."

Back then, my dad had told me a story that helped, at least for a while. He said he was driving across the floating bridge in Seattle when a rogue wave from Lake Washington crashed across his windshield, completely blinding his view. But he didn't slam on the brakes or swerve. He held the wheel straight and trusted the view would clear.

He said faith is like that. When your vision disappears, don't veer. Hold fast and keep moving in the direction of grace.

Dad said to imagine a "doubt basket" in my mind. Somewhere to place the questions that didn't have answers. "Put them in the basket, Ryan. Keep walking in the direction of Jesus. Trust that someday it will make sense."

And for years, I did exactly that.
The basket got fuller and fuller, but I kept walking.

Until now. Now I had time and space to set down the basket. I had a few hours alone in my office on a Tuesday to actually open the lid. And what I found was…heavy.

The questions weren't hypothetical anymore. They had faces.

They were coming from real people—people who showed up every week looking for answers, not platitudes. For honesty, not spiritual bypassing.

They were looking for God.

They asked about their gay son. Their Muslim neighbor. Their disillusioned adult daughter. And every time someone asked, "Is it okay to wonder about…?" something in me nodded. Because they were asking my questions too.

The same ones I'd been asking since junior high.
The same ones I tucked under theology.
The same ones I tried to bury with busyness.

People had warned me about the slippery slope. They said once you start questioning one thing—just one—you'll end up questioning everything. You'll lose your grip. You'll slide right into heresy, moral relativism, maybe even Unitarian potlucks.

So I didn't slide away easily. Before I ever let go of belief, I doubled down on it.

It's kind of sad and funny now to remember the season I launched into a multi-part sermon series about Old Testament prophecies "fulfilled by Jesus." The classic evangelical proof-text package. Messianic bingo. I knew the material—everyone did. Micah 5:2. Isaiah 7:14. Psalm 22. Daniel's seventy weeks. Prophecies we were told no one else could fulfill.

But deep down, I knew the arguments were thin.
I knew the cultural context was misunderstood.
I knew the logic only worked if you squinted hard and read it in English.

And still, I preached it. Passionately. I loaded those sermons like cannonballs and fired them across the stage—not because I was sure, but because I wasn't. I was out of integrity. My words were not my own.

Definitely not the beliefs. It was performative spirituality. If I could act certain long enough, maybe it would become real again.

I wasn't trying to manipulate anyone. I was trying to hold myself together. Trying to stay faithful to something I hoped was still true.

Because part of me still thought: What if this is a test?

What if all the honest doubt, all the ache, all the silence—was the final boss?
The last obstacle before breakthrough?
My personal dark night of the soul before reemerging victorious, a walking sermon illustration? Proof that I never wavered?

Maybe, just maybe, if I could hold on long enough, God would show up like he always does in the testimonies. Maybe I'd write a book about faithfulness in the wilderness. *How I Doubted Everything but Stayed True.* Maybe I'd get to stand up one day and say, "I never gave up, and now I see clearly."

Because the truth is that I wasn't trying to get out. I was trying to go deeper. To stay faithful. To live with integrity inside the tradition I was handed.

I figured if I stuck with it—kept reading the Bible, kept preaching, kept loving people, kept laying my life down for the church—God would show up. That belief would finally become experience.

But what I started to notice—quietly, and then unmistakably—was that I was doing all the right things, and something was still missing.

Sometimes it seemed like God might be there; other times it felt like I was talking to the ceiling. Sometimes prayer came through; other times, it felt like a coin toss. Sometimes the Bible offered a real insight; other times it read like ancient violence wrapped in religious insulation. And the people who claimed the most certainty often seemed the most afraid.

Eventually I started to think:
What if the slope is real, and I'm already on it?
Not because I stopped believing.
But because I started letting myself ask the questions my faith said I shouldn't need to ask.

Even in the early days, I used to tell the church, "I don't know if any of this is true. I was born in 1978. How would I know? The Jesus way just seems to *work*. Like, pragmatically. And until I have a better bet, I'm going with this."

It was honesty, not cynicism. I hadn't vetted these claims. I inherited them. Like a family recipe I'd never questioned because the casserole always showed up hot. But eventually, I had to ask: Did I actually believe this? Or was I just scared not to?

For me, the slide started with the doctrine of hell. I just couldn't reconcile that belief with the God I had grown to love. Eternal conscious torment for finite choices made by broken people born into complex stories? How did that square with love that "never fails"?

I didn't lose my theology overnight. I reluctantly edited it—like someone trying to preserve a photo album by tearing out the pages that gave them nightmares.

Then came the Bible. The Bible was supposed to be a living, breathing love letter from God. But when I read it with my eyes open, I saw genocide, misogyny, slavery, nationalism. I still saw beauty too. But it wasn't inerrant. It was human. Inspired, maybe, but not infallible.

I had always thought inspired meant dictated. Maybe "inspired" was more like the way heartbreak inspires a pop song.

And the slope steepened.

Next came sexuality. Then science. Then interfaith friendship. Then the realization that maybe people outside our religion already knew God in ways we refused to acknowledge.

I was just following the thread.
I was trying to stay true to what was real.

I used to say to our church, "If this thing is real, it should be able to handle the questions. If it can't—then maybe it was never as solid as we thought."

And I meant it.

I was trying to be honest. I desperately wanted to stay in the faith— but I wanted *my whole self* to fit into that faith. Not the disconnected, disembodied, fractured version of me I had been taught faith required, but the true me. The real me.

I didn't find clarity, though. I found a crack in the earth beneath me that grew wider and wider. There was the world I knew—structured, scriptural, safe in its promises. And there was the widening space of honesty, of terrifying openness, where the ground gave way and I was in danger of falling, with nothing to hold on to but the sky stretched endlessly above me.

I stood there for a long time.
Split.
Hoping the crack would close.
Hoping God would tell me where to stand.
Hoping belief would come back like solid ground.

But there was nothing but silence. The same silence that I felt as a teenager in church.

Now, just to be clear, this story wasn't playing out in a vacuum. It wasn't me, alone in a room, reading weird theology and having private doubts.

At the same time I was placing a tentative foot on the slippery slope and wondering what might happen if I let myself be truly honest, I was also part of something vibrant. Something real. Something so full of goodness I couldn't even dream of walking away from it.

The truth is, sermons were such a small part of what made our church work. What people came for and stayed for was the community.

It was a grace place.
A soft space in a hard world.
A pause in the middle of the week to bow down at the beauty of each and every human being.

We weren't perfect. But we said we were there for each other, and we meant it. We honored grief. We built systems to meet each other in lack. We showed up in times of illness, addiction, depression, divorce. We celebrated wins. We told the truth. We laughed—a lot.

And the people I got to do that with—my staff—were my best friends. Not theologians or religious professionals. Just people of love and joy.

People with wide hearts and sharp humor. I didn't hire from seminaries—I hired from life. From compassion. From character. And I still believe they are some of the most extraordinary human beings I've ever known.

Part of my job, more than preaching, was protecting that culture.

I spent most of my energy shielding our community from religious bullshit. The gatekeeping. The judgment. The shame. The performance. I worked hard to make sure EastLake was a place where you didn't have to pretend. Where you could be in process. Where you could be fully human without being disqualified from belonging.

But once we started booming, that got trickier. We weren't only attracting the spiritually curious—we were attracting a lot of Christians who loved the warmth, levity, and vitality of the place but wanted us to do some things like their last church. Less profanity. More dress code. Could I preach more "Bible-heavy" messages again? Could we tone down the edginess a bit?

They were drawn to the freedom, but they were nervous without the fences.

And I get it. Change is disorienting. But we weren't trying to recreate what existed down the road. We were trying to build something we hadn't seen yet. And it was exhilarating.

So no, I didn't launch myself down the slippery slope quickly or even willingly.

First, I stayed.
I stayed because something beautiful was happening.
I stayed because I wanted it to be true.

41

I stayed because I believed that honesty, grace, and love could hold it all together.
I stayed as long as I could—and then some.

Eventually, years later, I would realize the slippery slope wasn't a threat. It was an invitation.

They weren't wrong about the slope.
But they were wrong about the ride.
Because it's been fantastic, and I wouldn't change it for anything.

The fun part would come later, though.
First, the ground had to give way beneath my feet.

CHAPTER 7
THE UNRAVELING

"For authentic transformation is not a matter of belief but of the death of the believer; not a matter of translating the world but of transforming the world; not a matter of finding meaning but of being crushed by meaning. The self is not made content; the self is made toast."

—Ken Wilber

"The bad news is you're falling through the air, nothing to hang on to, and no parachute. The good news is, there is no ground."

—Chögyam Trungpa Rinpoche

I remember one time I was driving with my friend Fred out to go tubing on the Wenatchee River. It was about a two-hour drive, and somewhere around the halfway point, I started feeling terrible. Feverish, dizzy, sweating through my shirt. I was convinced I was getting the flu, maybe food poisoning. I was afraid I'd have to bail on the whole day.

Then I looked down and realized I'd accidentally turned the seat heater on full blast.

I wasn't sick. I was slow-roasting my own ass.

That story is a kind of parable. Sometimes, you're not breaking down. You're just stuck in a system that's slowly cooking you, and you haven't noticed yet. By the time the symptoms show up, you assume you're the problem—but only because the heat rose so slowly.

That's how I felt as I continued to lead a church while everything inside me was coming apart. Some days I could feel it physically—like a weight in my chest, a tightness in my throat. Other times it showed up as low-grade dread or a sadness I couldn't place.

I chalked it up to stress. The pressure of leading a growing, increasingly complex organization. And I kept going. Kept praying. Kept working. Kept pretending the warmth was holy, not harmful. That the heat meant I was doing it right.

But the temperature was rising. And it wasn't just emotional. Mostly, it was theological.

It started with the Bible.
More specifically, with the question:
"What is this book... really?"

I used to believe it was perfect. Inerrant. Infallible. The very breath of God, pressed into onion-skin pages and delivered to me with leather-bound certainty.

I believed it because I was told to. Because everyone around me did, including good people I loved and who really loved me. Because it gave structure to an otherwise chaotic and mysterious world. It made me feel safe.

And when it didn't make sense—when a story sounded cruel or a command felt off—I learned to gaslight myself.
To assume the problem was me, not the text.
Questioning meant I didn't understand God's holiness.
My discomfort was just human pride bumping up against divine wisdom.
I learned to override my instincts.
I learned to mistrust my own sense of right and wrong.

Growing up, I had assumed Bible college would be the place where the questions would finally be taken seriously. Where I'd find mentors who could help me bridge the gaps. I wasn't trying to tear anything down—I just wanted to understand. To go deeper. To hold onto my faith in a way that felt honest.

So when I went to college and started asking about divine violence, or why Paul sometimes sounds like a bitter gatekeeper, or why women had to be silent in church, I wasn't trying to undermine anything. I just wanted someone to help it make sense.

But the answers I got felt small. Recycled. Defensive.

Still, I didn't take that as a sign the Bible was flawed.
I took it as a sign I needed better guides.
More honest theologians. Wiser mentors.
Someone, somewhere, must be able to make it hold.

Now, as the pastor of a church, I was still committed to protecting the Bible. I just wasn't going to do it by stopping my questions.

Why does God seem so different in different books?
Why is there so much sanctioned violence?
Why are women so often property or afterthoughts?
Why does the New Testament command slaves to obey their masters?
Why does God sometimes sound more like a jealous warlord than the Jesus I'm trying to follow?

I think I was already standing inside what Dr. Greg Boyd calls a "house of cards" theology. The whole thing depended on every part staying perfectly intact. One contradiction, one failed prophecy, one morally indefensible command—and the structure started to wobble.

At the foundation of that house was a perfect, infallible Bible. Without that, the entire belief system felt like it would collapse.

Which meant that my sincere questions were more than theological—they were existential. When I asked what a problematic passage meant, I was unknowingly tugging on load-bearing beams.

One year, feeling spiritually disconnected and desperate for something to ground me, I resolved to stop reading anything except the Bible. No commentaries. No study guides. Just scripture. I told myself I would let the Word speak to me directly—pure and undiluted—trusting that the Holy Spirit would reveal truth.

That made things much worse.

On one hand, I saw the same beauty I'd always appreciated: the tenderness of the Psalms, the radical compassion of Jesus, the poetry of Isaiah. Those passages shimmered with love and mercy right beside the violence. If it had all been ugly, I would've left long before. But the beauty kept me hoping it could still be true.

On the other hand, when I finally let myself be honest, I kept encountering texts that made me cringe. Commands I couldn't square with goodness. Portraits of God that felt abusive, erratic, even cruel. And instead of brushing them aside or spiritualizing them away, I started a file on my laptop, a literal Word document titled something like "Circle Back: Disturbing Stuff God Apparently Said."

It became a running log of everything I couldn't explain away. A digital version of the mental "doubt basket" I'd been told to use, now with footnotes.

When I finished Revelation, the last book of the Bible, I realized I felt even more alienated than when I started.

So, naturally, I began again.
From the top.
Genesis. Exodus. Leviticus.
Another full read-through.
More verses. More questions.
The file kept growing.

That was the most I ever read the Bible, before or since. Needless to say, the second round didn't help. The document just got longer.

1 Samuel 15 was one of many horrific landmines: "Thus says the LORD of hosts.… 'Do not spare them, but kill both man and woman, child and infant, ox and sheep, camel and donkey.'"

Entire populations—men, women, children, animals—slaughtered. Not by human vengeance. By divine order. What do you do with that if you believe the Bible is God's literal voice?

Exodus 32 was violence directed at their own people. "This is what the LORD, the God of Israel, says: 'Each of you men is to fasten his sword to his side, go back and forth through the camp from gate to gate, and slay his brother, his friend, and his neighbor.'"

We would call this barbarism in any other sacred text.
A grotesque, if not diabolical, conception of God.

I'm not going to catalogue every disturbing verse. There are so many, and that task is beyond the scope of this book—and honestly, beyond my interest these days. If you're in the mood for a full inventory, there are lots of other books, or some determined Reddit thread has you covered.

But because these verses are in the Bible, Christians are told they're holy no matter how monstrous, unjust, illogical, or contradictory they are.

If a portrait of God would've been less beautiful had he refrained from orchestrating genocide, then the word *beauty* no longer means anything.

Indeed, many Western Christians today denounce Islam as violent and blame the Quran. But the Bible raises considerably more issues in terms of bloodshed, divine wrath, and sanctioned cruelty.

I remember pissing some folks off one Sunday when I told everyone I was going to read some of the violent texts from the Quran. I let them sit and soak in the horror of each one and then revealed to everyone that each line I had just read was actually from the Bible.

Not everyone appreciated that.

If we don't confront these portrayals honestly—if we don't stop sacralizing cruelty and calling it holiness—then our religion becomes not a wellspring of life, but a loaded weapon.

When we divorce holiness from goodness and goodness from decency, we've lost the plot. And when we hand divine authority to every command, every curse, every wartime decree, we baptize some of the worst ideas humans have ever had.

Slavery was justified with the Bible.
So was colonialism.
So was misogyny.
So was racism.
So was genocide.
So was religious war.
So was homophobia.

When I voiced these concerns, I was handed the usual balm: *"God's ways are higher than our ways."*

I used to say it too.

But eventually, I couldn't anymore. Because if God's ways are higher, shouldn't they also be better? Kinder? More loving than the tribal morality of Iron Age people? More just than the ethics of slaveholding empires? More compassionate than war chants and purity codes and blood rituals?

The violence in the Bible wasn't the only thing that tripped me up.
There was also the ordinariness.
The smallness.
The glaring absence of anything that might suggest this book came from a being with access to all time.

No mention of germs or galaxies. No guidance on things like the immune system, trauma, or even basic hygiene that wasn't already common sense at the time. Nothing about DNA, electricity, the structure of the solar system, or the makeup of the oceans. But somehow, there was exhaustive detail on livestock protocols and exactly how to acquire and manage your slaves.

Sure, there's moral guidance—but most of it reflects the values of the culture it came from. Which makes sense *if* the Bible is what it appears to be: an ancient text, written by ancient people, limited by their ancient worldview. Not a divine download. Not a cosmic blueprint. Just the spiritual literature of a small, struggling tribe trying to make sense of their suffering and survival.

Even the details give it away. The Bible's authors describe the earth as flat, the sky as a solid dome, and measurements that only make sense if you're eyeballing it from the ground. It doesn't sound like the voice of a cosmic engineer—it sounds like what it is: a human attempt to make sense of reality with the tools of its time.

Once I could see it that way, the spell broke. Because if this was the best an all-knowing being could offer—a collection of scrolls without a single insight that wouldn't have been known to Iron Age people—then omniscience must be a lot more disappointing than I thought.

The more I studied it, the more the structure cracked. The texts weren't unified; they were layered, edited, and contradictory. The morality wasn't transcendent; it was tribal, patriarchal, and violent in the same ways other ancient cultures were violent. The history didn't hold up under scrutiny, either, because archaeology and textual criticism exposed gaps, inventions, and revisions. Even the idea of a single divine voice collapsed under the weight of multiple theologies arguing inside the same book.

Then there was the issue of how the canon itself was debated, contested, and stitched together over centuries—how politics and power shaped which writings were called sacred and which were buried or burned. How the New Testament's central symbols—virgin birth, divine sonship, resurrection—had already circulated for centuries in older Hellenistic and Persian myths. It became harder to pretend this was a unique divine revelation rather than part of a long human tradition of mythmaking and meaning-making. What I'd been taught to call "God's Word" began to look less like a message delivered from heaven and more like a collective record of our species groping toward transcendence.

And even if I could look past all that—if I could still believe this book came from God—I'd have to deal with an even trickier problem: What kind of God does it actually reveal?

Now I was dealing with more than a credibility problem. This was a character issue.

And that brought me to the next question—the one hiding behind almost every version of salvation I'd ever heard: How good is good enough?

I remember that question burning into my head one time when I attended a funeral because the guy being eulogized had been, frankly, an asshole—but everyone was confidently proclaiming, "We know he's with Jesus now." Why? Because he was a card-carrying member of the Christian faith.

I smirked and thought, *Well, if he's going to heaven, then I guess everyone's going!*

Now, I know the evangelical response to that would be something like, "It's not about being a good person. It's grace. Even the most moral person needs the saving grace of Jesus through the cross."

They frame it like it's good news because it doesn't matter how good or bad you are. But what they're really saying is that in place of being good through behavior, all you need to do is be good through belief—to accept the so-called gift by assenting to the correct theology.

That shift from correct behavior to correct belief doesn't free anyone. It just swaps one set of conditions for another, turning what's supposedly an unconditional gift into a psychological ransom.

You're not judged on how you live (which might actually help the real world). Instead, you're judged on whether you believe a specific theological narrative.

And that allows you to remain an asshole.

I finally realized that right *belief* isn't any less of a condition than right *behavior*. If we're going to talk about divine grace, if we're going to suggest there's truly good news for everyone, then it has to be universal.

It's for everyone, or it's not grace.

And anyway, that's not even how belief works. You can't force yourself to believe something. Belief happens when something seems plausible—when it aligns with your understanding of reality.

If I offered you a million dollars to believe that your bones are made of 24-karat gold, even if you wanted to believe it, you probably couldn't. Based on everything you know about human biology—and the weight of gold—it just wouldn't pass the plausibility test.

Your only real option would be to pretend.

Or worse, to fracture yourself until you *can* believe the implausible— not because it's true, but because if you don't, a gracious, loving God will have no choice but to roast you in hell forever.
He doesn't want to, of course.
He just makes the rules.

You can see why some people feel there's a lot riding on convincing themselves to believe, or at least pretending to believe.

For me, the game was growing old, and the cognitive dissonance was getting exhausting.

But the machine itself was still going strong.

CHAPTER 8
JUKEBOX PREACHER

"It's hard to listen while you preach."

—Bono

Sunday kept coming. The slide had started, but the machine hadn't stopped.

Even as my inner world was coming apart, the church was still growing. People kept showing up with real needs and real wounds. And I loved them. I still believed in grace, in beauty, in the redemptive potential of community and love and becoming.

But I couldn't say what was really happening in me—not yet. I couldn't risk it. We were a success story, and I had to keep the momentum up. People didn't want to hear about my existential crisis; they wanted a word from God.

I felt like a jukebox. People dropped in their donation and expected a familiar tune. So I played the hits—old sermons I'd recycled from earlier years, or hand-me-down sermons from my dad and mentors. Something biblical. Something comforting. Something funny, but still holy. Something challenging, but not too much. Something that gave answers without raising new questions.

Play the hits, keep them singing, and don't ask questions.

What made it harder is that the thing we were doing was actually working. While I was wrestling with long-held questions about my faith, EastLake was thriving.

The years 2011-2014 were our golden era.

We launched five new campuses in a single weekend and eventually grew to eight. The staff was growing—fun, energetic, deeply bonded— and our community was alive with generosity and vision. The church was working, and it was beautiful. We had momentum. People were growing, healing, changing.

By every measurable metric, we were crushing it.

We even hosted two benefit concerts at our largest location. No preaching, no offerings, no self-promotion. Just Saturday night shows with live music, pulled pork sandwiches, and enough kegs to serve a baseball stadium. All sales and donations went directly to global clean water projects. The energy was powerful and so damn fun.

And all the while, people were making decisions to follow Jesus. Small groups were multiplying. Leaders were stepping up. The staff culture felt like rare magic—lifelong friendships forming in real time. We laughed our asses off. We celebrated each other's wins. We worked hard, and we loved the work. We believed in what we were building. And even more than that, we loved each other.

In fact, the real engine underneath everything was the way this team of best friends showed up for the mission and for each other with unshakable trust. We had found something real.

If you ask most people who were part of it, they'll tell you:
"Those were the IT years. The high point."

And they were.

What was strange (but paradoxically almost cruel) is that this season holds some of the most beautiful moments in my ministry. Watching someone's face light up as they realized they were actually safe. Watching a room of strangers become a family. Watching our team evolve— become more compassionate, more courageous, more themselves. The grace we created together felt real.

But the more I talked with people in our community, the more I realized they were carrying the same cognitive dissonance I was. They were wondering about their gay children. Their Buddhist neighbors. Their own ability to believe supernatural Bible stories anymore. They were living lives full of love and complexity and contradiction while quietly trying to make peace with the God we'd been taught was watching.

What was really hard was they had the same questions I'd carried since I was a teenager. Since Bible college. Since my late-night Word doc of disturbing passages.

Only now I was the one expected to answer them.
To speak with clarity about things that no longer felt clear.

And I started to wonder:
What if the God we built this whole thing around was too small for this?
What if we needed a bigger story?

I remember one night in 2012 at one of the big events we'd put together during that stretch when everything felt alive. The room was full. There was laughter, movement, real excitement in the air. It wasn't fake, showbiz energy. Just people who were glad to be together, doing something that felt like it mattered.

A few minutes before it all began, I pulled the band in. They were some of my closest friends, still holding guitars, fiddling with pedalboards, checking cables. We stood in a loose circle near the edge of the stage.

And I said, "Remember this moment. Enjoy it. It won't last. Nothing does. So be here fully. Feel it. I love you guys."

I didn't say that because I knew what was coming.
I just felt the sun shining, and I wanted us to feel it together.

But maybe—underneath the words—something in me was already whispering that a storm was coming.
Maybe that moment was a premonition.
Maybe I sensed, even then, that we were standing in something special.
Something that wouldn't last.

Not long after that, we spent a weekend at a friend's lake house. It was everything a summer weekend at the lake should be: boats and sunshine, our kids sprinting across the grass, music playing somewhere behind the screen door. We grilled meat. We jumped off docks. We laughed hard. The air filled with the scent of sunscreen and wood decks.

One afternoon I wandered down to the dock with a Rainier in one hand and a book I definitely wasn't supposed to be reading in the other—something by Brian McLaren, I think, or another one of those authors people used to warn me about. I wasn't looking to make any decisions that day. I just couldn't *not* read it anymore.

Unfortunately, it was making too much sense.

Not just intellectually or theologically, but personally. It was speaking directly to the parts of me I had been avoiding. The ones I kept buried under busyness and sermons and responsibility. It was like someone had written a letter to the version of me I didn't know how to admit I'd become.

And sitting there, beer in hand, sun slipping behind the trees, I felt it—a creeping dread. Like stale air in a sealed room or something rotting in the cellar.

Everything around me was beautiful. Easy. Carefree.
Meanwhile, something knowing in me whispered:
Oh. I'm fucked.

It was the first real moment I let myself realize this wasn't a phase, or a test, or a trial to push through. There by the lake, I finally admitted the truth I'd been avoiding.

When it came to the faith I'd been given, the faith I'd preached and explained and defended and wrestled with, I didn't believe all of it.
I didn't believe most of it, in fact.
Or maybe…any of it.
I really didn't know.

I just knew it wasn't right.
It wasn't honest.
It wasn't good.
And it wasn't working.

CHAPTER 9

COMING OUT

"You can stand up for anything that you believe in.
But if you can't find the courage to stand alone,
it won't really matter what you believe."
– Stacie Martin

My first move wasn't exactly public, but it was a step in that direction. It was a conversation I had been avoiding for months.

I told Michelle.

I don't remember exactly how I said it.
Just that it was terrifying. And long overdue.

I told her I wasn't sure what I believed anymore.
That I wasn't trying to walk away from faith, but the God I'd been handed didn't make sense to me anymore.
That I was struggling.
And that I was afraid she'd leave the marriage over this.

To her credit—God, to her credit—she didn't run. She didn't lash out or walk away. But she was scared. We both knew we were toying with a bomb of sorts. For years, our whole life had been built around this shared story of faith and ministry; questioning it felt like pulling a thread that could unravel everything.

It took time. Weeks of uneasy conversations, long silences, late-night talks that ended in tears. She needed space to breathe through the fear and decide if she could even stay open to where I was headed. But slowly, bravely, she did.

Eventually, she told me she'd been carrying many of the same doubts. That for a long time she'd been too afraid to really look at them—afraid of where it would all lead, afraid of losing everything. We could also see how privilege had sheltered us from even needing to ask certain questions. Our theology worked for us. We didn't have a trans kid, or friends whose faith or culture pushed ours to the edges. We hadn't buried a child or faced the kind of senseless loss that makes tidy answers feel cruel.

But once this was all out in the open and we could look at it honestly, Michelle moved faster than I did.

Especially when we got to the LGBTQ+ conversation.

For me, that was still a minefield. I had read dozens of books and articles on both sides—maybe seventy by that point. I had mapped the Greek, parsed the context, traced every clobber verse into exhaustion. It was pretty clear by then that I didn't have to abandon Scripture to affirm my gay friends. And still I was terrified to say out loud what I already felt was true.

Because I knew what would come next: a holy shitstorm. We were an evangelical megachurch, for God's sake.

But for Michelle, it was simple.
"They're fine," she said. "They're wonderful. I don't need to read a book to see that."

She wasn't dismissive. She was just clear.
Clearer than I was.
And that clarity humbled me.

Because the thing I was dragging my soul through—defending, dissecting, delaying—she just saw. And named. And accepted. I didn't even know that it was an option to trust my own read and be done with it.

Soon after that, we began talking about it as a church staff. The conversations were honest but divided. Some were afraid we were drifting too far. Others were urging me to evolve more quickly and more publicly, to stop hiding, to lead.

My heart was already there.
But I was scared to go first.
Scared of what it would cost.
Scared that if I named it all out loud, the whole thing would come crashing down.

And then a staff member came out.
They were terrified we'd fire them.
Someone we loved.
Someone faithfully doing the work of the church.

That was it for me.

This wasn't about policy or doctrine. This was about people, and fear, and the harm we were doing by staying silent.

It was time to tell the truth.

I gathered the whole staff. I told them: "I'm going to take a public stance. This won't go well. We may all lose our jobs. If you need to vote me off the island, now's the time."

I asked them to vote anonymously. I didn't want anyone to feel pressured. This had to be real and honest.

When the votes came in, it was unanimous. "We're in."
Every single one of them.

This little team of misfit toys.
They stood with me—not because it was safe, but because it was right.
Because we loved each other.
Because we were willing to fall as a team if that's what it took.
We were gonna burn this thing down together.

I'll never forget that.

In the summer of 2014, my parents came up for a visit. One afternoon, my dad and I were in the woods behind our house in a tree fort my friend Andy had built high in the evergreens, with a view of the Olympics on a clear day.

We sat up there in the stillness. Just us.

I told him what I was planning. That I was going to speak publicly about LGBTQ+ inclusion and that it could cost me everything.

Then I asked the question I was scared to know the answer to: "Do you think I'm crazy? Dangerous? Leading people astray? Should I resign? Disappear?"

He didn't rush to answer. He took a deep breath, leaned back on the wooden bench, and looked through the trees.

Then he said, "Ryan, I trust you. You already know this isn't going to make your life easier. It's going to cost you a lot. We may not see this the same way, but I know you're coming from a deeply good place in your heart."

For all the pain that had come—and all that was still ahead—that one affirmation from my childhood hero kept me afloat.

We planned to make our public announcement in February. In December, I flew to New York. I was visiting an episcopal seminary and reconnecting with a few friends in town when my phone rang.

First it was *TIME* Magazine. A journalist had been tipped off—someone told her I was gay-affirming. She reached out to see if it was true.

I told her: "We haven't made a public statement yet, but yes. We're planning to go public soon. I'm happy to answer your questions."

It felt honest. Measured. I didn't think much of it.

Then another call came. A very well-known megachurch pastor. A household name. He'd heard I was making a shift on this topic, and he wanted to talk.

I braced myself, expecting a rebuke. But it never came.

He was kind.
Curious.
Almost relieved to have someone to talk to about it.

He told me he had many of the same concerns. That he wasn't sure how long he could keep quiet. That he had people on staff he loved who were wrestling too. That he didn't know what to do, but he saw the problem.

It shocked me.

How many pastors feel the same way but haven't said anything? Preaching sermons they no longer believe because they're afraid of what honesty might cost?

That call steeled my resolve.
This wasn't just about me.
This was a dam waiting to break.

Then, in mid-January, Michelle and I were in the airport on our way to Omaha to visit friends. I stopped in a Hudson News store to grab a snack, and there it was.

The TIME Magazine issue.

The headline on the cover read: "Inside the Evangelical Fight Over Gay Marriage."

I flipped it open and saw my name. My picture. My quotes. My voice.

"I refuse to go to a church where my friends who are gay are excluded."

And then, near the end of the article,

"Every positive reforming movement in church history is first labeled heresy. Evangelicalism is way behind on this. We have a debt to pay."

It was all out there now.
The past.
The wound.
The reckoning.
The plan.

And it was out early, a full week ahead of our announcement. My blood ran cold.

The calls started immediately. People were freaking out. Panicking. Angry. Disappointed. Confused. A childhood friend who had already left the church years earlier called to rebuke me, furious we were even talking about social justice at all.

Online, it got worse.
Social media lit up with arguments.
People defending us.
People attacking us.

People I loved—people I had vacationed with, officiated weddings for, started the church with—were now airing every frustration they'd ever had, no punches pulled. The pot was boiling.

I flew back and recorded a video that was part sermon, part announcement, and part apology on Thursday. We were a multi-site church, and I always taped the message midweek for all campuses.

By Saturday, everything was getting out of control.

I was spinning out.
The pressure. The pain. The accusations.
It was too much.

I recorded a video for our staff, asking them not to defend me or the church online. *Let people speak. Stay grounded. Stay loving. We knew this wouldn't go over easy.*

Then, my former boss—another pastor who'd once prophesied at a leadership retreat that Michelle and I would one day start a church—called and asked to meet. He came to my office and pleaded with me to reverse course. He told me I was making a huge mistake and said there was still time to fix it.

I tried to hear him. To stay calm and kind, but also to be clear.

He just pushed harder. When he finally left, he told me I was deceived. He warned me that this was a massive failure of leadership and I would regret it.

And after the door closed, I broke down. Completely. I couldn't stop crying. I was afraid to go home and let my kids see me like that.

Another pastor friend came over to console me. He sat with me, listened, and embraced me. He told me he supported me and reminded me I was loved.

Later that night, I found out he called Michelle and told her I looked unstable. He cautioned her not to leave me alone.

A doctor friend prescribed some anti-anxiety meds to help me rest, but they didn't help. I barely slept.

Sunday morning was staring me down.

CHAPTER 10
THE STORM

"I have fallen in love with the world,
and I am aware that I have chosen
the most dangerous companion possible."
—Nina Riggs, *The Bright Hour*

"The loneliest moment in someone's life is when they are
watching their whole world fall apart,
and all they can do is stare blankly."
—F. Scott Fitzgerald

The message went live on Sunday morning, streamed to all our campuses and posted online.

My voice, my face, my conviction—all of it now archived and untakebackable. It was the sermon I had recorded a few days earlier: our public stance of full LGBTQ+ inclusion. The one where I said out loud what I could no longer contain. The one that began with an apology for my complicit silence in the stigmatization and marginalization of parts of our community. The one that ended with their clear affirmation, celebration, and inclusion in the full life of our community.

Surprisingly, the room responded with a standing ovation. I was glad. I appreciated it. But I was under no illusion that everyone approved. I remember one family gathered their kids and walked out halfway through, shaking their heads. Others sat stunned in their seats. Some cried. Some cheered. Most stood and applauded.

The announcement roared across our campuses that morning like a tornado barreling through an unsuspecting town. And by noon, debris was falling everywhere. Emails. Phone calls. Facebook rants. Members demanding to speak with me directly. Elders from other churches calling to offer correction.

I had thought the thunderstorm would hit all at once. But it was more like a series, each one crashing over me as I was still picking up the pieces from the last.

Some of the messages were tough.
"You're leading people straight to hell."
"You've betrayed us all."
"I can't believe we trusted you."

Others were deeply encouraging.
"My daughter just came out last year, and your words gave me hope."
"Thank you. I never thought I'd see the day."
"I wept through the whole message. You have no idea what this means to me."

And then there were the silent ones—the long-time members who just vanished. No goodbye. No note. Just…gone.

In the weeks that followed, everything accelerated. We hosted two weekend-long events we called "Together in This," which were intentional spaces to bring people along in our process. We brought in theologians, doctors, writers, and LGBTQ+ voices from around the world to share stories, challenge assumptions, and model a different kind of conversation. People begged us to reconsider. Others begged us to go further. Some came to scream. Others came to sob.

Donations to the church dropped almost immediately. That whole year, our financial controller was on the phone with people canceling their giving. We were hemorrhaging.

Volunteers disappeared. A few staff members, realizing this was going to be a bigger deal than they thought, decided to resign.

My staff and I were flooded with coffee appointments. Conversations that were supposed to be relational check-ins turned into exhausting debates about the Bible. It felt like that's all we did for months—field arguments, parse scripture, try to hold space for people's fears while standing firm in our integrity.

And not only with those who disagreed. Even people who supported our decision came with their own questions:
How far are you really going with this?
What about weddings?
What about leadership roles?

I had tried my best in the sermon to be clear: "You don't have to see this exactly like I do to be part of this church. But we will not exclude. Not in policy, not in silence, not by omission. People need to know they are safe here. Not just tolerated until some future debate, but embraced *now*."

I wasn't going to let someone sign up for membership only to later find out we wouldn't marry them, welcome their partner, or allow them to lead. If people were going to leave, I wanted them to leave based on full transparency, not because of ambiguity or bait-and-switch theology.

It was striking to realize that many who expressed outrage over my public change of heart had never actually confronted a gay person about their supposed sin. They weren't picketing pride parades or refusing to officiate weddings. But they sure as hell wanted to make sure I would do the fighting, the judging, and the excluding on their behalf.

One big realization that year was that the reason people stay in a church often has less to do with theology and more to do with community. Plenty of people agreed with our position but left anyway simply because their friends left. For others, it was because their family life became a war zone, with religious parents berating them for attending such a "sinful church." They didn't need the battle.

And here's the part the critics never seem to get: This wasn't some clever growth strategy. Fundamentalists love to accuse progressive churches of compromising truth to be more "worldly," as if non-Christians are just waiting in the wings for us to tweak some theology so they can join up.

HA.

Sure, some new folks came and found our shift healing. But by 2015, most of American culture had already moved on from this conversation.

We weren't ahead—we were late.
We weren't relevant—we were waking up in public.
And we weren't trailblazers—we were the hillbillies finally catching up to reality.

So no, we didn't swell with eager new members. We didn't win a new crowd. As Michelle said at one point, "Back then, we thought we were the good ones—opening the doors to welcome others into our great, enlightened thing. But what we learned was that love was already out there, alive and free. We were the ones who needed to walk out and find it."

News articles started popping up in gay publications. *Upworthy* ran a feature on our announcement. I got a few death threats. Protestors set up out front. Christian prayer groups met on our front steps midweek and prayed against the "evil" influence of our church. Fundamentalist blogs lit up with "warnings" about our slide into heresy. And God knows, people were talking. I tried to tune it out, but stories kept finding their way to me—about social gatherings where we were getting shredded, about the latest blogs chronicling our downfall.

One local pastor called just to "chat." He wasn't there for conversation, though. He was there to correct me. I tried to stay kind, but it was obvious this wasn't pastoral care. It was a warning shot.

And then there were the secret meetings.

Behind the scenes, I was getting pulled into whispered conversations with other pastors—men (yes, almost always men) who quietly admitted they agreed with us. Who had read the same books, wrestled with the same scriptures, and landed in the same place. But they couldn't say it out loud.
"I'd lose my job."
"The board would fire me."
"The giving would disappear."

They wanted to be on the right side of history—but not yet. Not publicly. Not if it cost them what it was costing us.

I remember laughing to myself—tired, dry laughter—when people told me they were leaving our church over our "unbiblical stance," only to join churches where the pastors had personally confided in me they were in the same place, just unable to say so publicly.

I understood, though. Certainty is the evangelical currency. And I was broke.

People didn't want a pastor who was on a journey. You could have a story as long as it was in the past tense. You could share the valleys, the struggle, the wrestling as long as it was all resolved now. Tidy. Settled.

I didn't judge them. But I couldn't continue to be one of them.

It felt like that scene from *Raiders of the Lost Ark* where Indiana Jones steals the golden idol and instantly all hell breaks loose. That was us. We dared to touch the sacred talisman of evangelical theology, and suddenly the ground gave way. Traps sprung. Arrows flew. The giant boulder of institutional backlash came roaring after us. We weren't brave explorers—we were twitchy amateurs who'd triggered something ancient and unstable. And now we were running full speed, clutching this fragile truth. Like it would either save us or crush us before we made it out alive.

Somewhere in the middle of it all, I had a dream. Well, I had a *lot* of dreams, but one lodged itself deep in my bones.

I was behind the wheel of a massive truck barreling out of control. The brakes were gone. No matter what I did, I couldn't stop it. Eventually, I crashed into a towering wall made entirely of cages. Metal and wire, stacked and sprawling like a fortress. And from one of those cages, something was released.

A giant owl.

As it burst out, I looked up and realized I was being watched from some kind of observation tower, high above. The Powers that Be. Shadowy figures of authority. They had seen everything, and I knew instantly: I was in trouble. Deep trouble. They were coming.

I scrambled to catch the owl, to put it back, to undo whatever I had done and get the hell out of there. But it kept slipping through my hands. I was frantic. Panicked. The observers descended. They berated me, scolded me for what I had unleashed. I kept trying to trap the owl again, fix it, reverse it, pretend I hadn't opened anything.

But then the owl circled me…and landed on my left shoulder.

I stood frozen as its massive wings wrapped around my head, draping me in darkness.

And then—inside that darkness—I could see my own skull.

I woke up drenched in sweat.

Back then, I couldn't see past the nightmare. I was afraid I was losing my mind. But eventually I made peace with that owl. I came to know it as the emissary calling me deeper into my freefall. It's even on the cover of this book and tattooed on my arm. I came to realize that the "thing" I had unleashed by daring to think, to love, and to speak wasn't there to kill me, but to empower me.

It felt like death.

But that's because it was stripping me down to the rawest version of myself. To save my life and find my soul.

And yet, even then, between the nightly dreams and the daily arguments, for every door that closed, another opened.

People we'd never met started showing up. Couples arrived who had never felt safe in church. Elders from other churches snuck over with their queer kids. LGBTQ+ folks who had given up on Christianity years ago came by, just to see if we meant it.

They cried in the lobby. Sat in the back. Lit up when we remembered their names.

We were losing our church. And sort of becoming one.

I loved it, but it was still hell. I wasn't sleeping. I was grieving and managing and pastoring and falling apart all at once.

The adrenaline that had carried me into the announcement was gone now. I was left with dust and fragments. People stopped making eye contact in public. Some looked through me like I was dead.

And to be honest, part of me was. A version of me died in those months. The version that thought I could hold it all together. The version that believed integrity and charisma and a good heart would be enough.

They weren't.
At least not in the system I had built.

Throughout that year, we tried to stabilize. We consolidated campuses. Cut costs. Reworked staff roles. Held retreats to care for our team. But we were bleeding out.

Sometimes people go to therapy when one person walks out on them. That year, I watched thousands leave over just a few months. I told myself I was ready for it. I even believed it was what needed to happen. But knowing it's coming doesn't spare you from the ache of actually living through it.

What I didn't see until much later was how deeply that collective exodus got inside me. Because no matter how hard you try to stay humble, the ego gets fed when the numbers are up. It feels good to be "winning." And when those numbers start to fall, it's hard not to feel like you're losing.

For the next few years, we'd be on one hell of a losing streak. The truth is, there was fruit in the humiliation. I needed to learn how to separate my worth from how many people stuck around. To live out my values without the validation of the crowd. To learn that I could stand alone if I had to.

Before the split, on our peak Sunday, we had more than 8,000 attending across campuses. Within a year, we were gathering less than 2,000.

And still we kept grinding.

Still we sang. Still we loved each other. Still we passed the mic and shared stories and held space for joy and pain and holy disorientation.

And sometimes—on the best days—it felt like church.

The contrast was dizzying. On one hand: betrayal, slander, abandonment. Friends vanished. Support dried up. Some who had once championed our vision now treated us like a cautionary tale. On the other: letters, emails, tears of gratitude. People thanking us for saying what they didn't think any church would say. For saving their faith. For making space for their children. For themselves.

It was as if judgment and healing were happening side by side. A spiritual earthquake exposing what had always been underground.

There's a photo someone took in that season. I'm standing in front of our team during a midweek staff meeting with swollen eyes, holding a coffee mug with both hands like it's the only thing anchoring me to the earth.

I don't remember what I was saying. But I remember the look in my eyes: emptied, straining to stay present, hollowed out. Just hanging on.

In the middle of all the intensity swirling around us—while friendships shattered, conversations deteriorated into debates, and we fell further and further from the good graces of our religion—a staff member and my good friend Aaron Sternke wrote a song for his band, *Fell from a Star*. It was called "Madness," and it captured exactly what we were feeling:

> Love,
> Against the lines
> Fans the flame
> Draws the ire
> Starts a fight
> You and I
> Fade away
> Drift apart
>
> But if my only sin
> Was loving
> What good is goodness?
> What good is all this?
> And if the only right
> Is a half life
> Then I choose madness
> It's all I've got left

I choose madness.

It wasn't rebellion or valor or arrogance—it was honesty.
Like someone standing in the wreckage of everything that once mattered and choosing aliveness anyway.

CHAPTER 11
THE LAST PRAYER

"Bless the thing that broke you down and cracked you open
because the world needs you open."
— Rebecca Campbell

"Hard is trying to rebuild yourself, piece by piece,
with no instruction book, and no clue to where all
the important bits are supposed to go."
—Nick Hornby

It was July of 2015. We were months into the fallout from our public statement of LGBTQ+ inclusion. The cost had landed, and I was crumbling.

My inbox, my Facebook feed, my chest—everything was tight. Every breath felt like it had to sneak past some kind of invisible weight pressing down on me. I was ragged, stretched thin across a thousand coffee appointments with people who wanted to lecture me about the Bible.

In the middle of all that mess a friend said, almost in passing: "You should talk to this guy I know. He's a medium. I think he could help you."

I laughed. *That's not me*, I thought. *That's not allowed.*

But the ache in my body was louder than my theology. And honestly, I didn't care about the rules anymore. I just wanted the pit in my stomach to go away. I wanted to feel something besides dread. I wanted help.

So I went.

Michelle and I sat across from a man I didn't know. I told him, "Look, I don't trust you, and I don't trust *me*, but if you can help me with this feeling in my gut, I'm open to it."

He smiled and said, "If you're asking if I work in the light—I do."

And instead of conning me, instead of theatrics, he simply…listened. He named exactly what was going on. He called out the specific pain I was carrying from a childhood friend who had wounded me deeply. I relaxed a little. Maybe this guy actually knew what he was doing.

He said a few more things he couldn't have known. He asked questions no one else dared to ask. And whatever was happening— whether it was real, metaphor, or mystery—I felt something uncoil in me that day.

Something ancient.
Something buried.
Something I didn't know could move.

He did some kind of energy work on me, and I could feel it, right in my center. I won't try to convince you it was real. If someone had told me this a year earlier, I wouldn't have believed them either. But I'm sure glad Michelle was there to witness it all too.

We left that meeting wide-eyed, a little dazzled, and curious about what else we didn't know about the world.

And I left without the pit.

It wasn't all fixed. But it led me into healing I'd been too indoctrinated in fear to consider.

Months later, in December 2015, I signed up for something called the Hoffman Process. I didn't know much about it—only that it was supposed to help you get to the root of your pain and rewrite the patterns you inherited from childhood.

I knew I needed it. Michelle and I both did.
We were exhausted.
And we didn't want to pass down what we were carrying to our kids.

I flew to California and arrived early. Before the program started, I walked into the small town of St. Helena to clear my head. As I wandered, I came across an old church.

I tried the door. It was unlocked.
The sanctuary was tiny. Empty.

I walked to the altar and, for some reason, I knelt. I hadn't prayed in a long time. Not like that. Not to the God I used to believe in. But something in me needed to speak.

"This is your last chance," I said. "If you are real, show up. I've tried so hard to know you. I've given you everything. But if you can't meet me here, now, then I'm out. I'm going to this thing partly to get over you. To heal from you. From the abusive silence I've spent my whole life trying to interpret as love."

And then I waited.

Nothing happened.
There was no reply. No inner voice. No warmth. Just silence.

But for once, it didn't scare me. It didn't even make me sad.
It felt ... honest. Final. A clearing.

And with that, I stood up.
And I walked out.

The Hoffman Process blew the doors off the rest of that year's grief.

For the first time in a long while, I felt almost normal. I was just one of thirty people sitting in a circle, all in pain, all showing up to see if something might help. Halfway through the week, I laughed—really laughed. I even played, like a kid. Some light was breaking in.

In those seven days, I raged. I wept. I danced. I breathed. I screamed into pillows.
I met parts of myself I had disowned in the name of faithfulness.
I was held, and seen, and loved. And I could breathe again.

It didn't fix the church, and I could still feel the pressure looming, but I was done grieving the fallout.
And I was done looking for the old God.
I let myself feel how angry I was at a God who I wasn't even sure existed anymore.

I came home lighter.
Not healed, but healing.
Not certain, but clear.

Michelle went the next week. She returned rejuvenated, alive, and hopeful.

We knew we were carrying too much, and we refused to hand it all to our kids. So we started there.

With a clearing. And a final prayer.
A space for something new.

PART 2
HEAVEN TO EARTH

CHAPTER 12
THE FIDELITY OF BETRAYAL

"What if one of the core demands of a radical Christianity lay
in a call for its betrayal, while the ultimate act of affirming God
required the forsaking of God? And what if fidelity to the Judeo-
Christian Scriptures demanded their renunciation? In short,
what would it mean if the only way of finding real faith involved
betraying it with a kiss?"
— Peter Rollins, *The Fidelity of Betrayal*

There's a long tradition in Judaism called *midrash*. It's the sacred practice of wrestling with the Scriptures. Of asking hard questions not to
destroy the faith, but to stay faithful to it.

That's what we were trying to do: be faithful to the deeper impulse
beneath it all. Author and philosopher Peter Rollins calls this "the fidelity of betrayal." It's the willingness to betray the surface form of religion
in order to stay loyal to its animating spirit.

During those next few years of rethinking faith on a very public stage,
that's exactly what we were doing. It felt like we had become the last
stop on the train out of Christianity. A methadone dispensary for those
weening off the high of evangelical fundamentalism. A soft landing
for people who still loved Jesus, or mystery, or maybe just community.

So we experimented. We hosted interfaith voices, including rabbis,
imams, Buddhists, humanists, mystics. We read from the Tao, from
Ram Dass, from evolutionary philosophers who saw the cosmos itself

as sacred. We sang songs that honored grief, wonder, longing; songs that didn't require belief to be true.

We were trying to distill something essential. To offer the best of what religion can be, without the fear, the certainty, or the superiority. We wanted to live in the questions and still call it church.

During that time, people came out of the woodwork. Some just to see the spectacle—maybe to confirm their suspicions of heresy. But others came quietly, curiously. Leaders from other churches would pull me aside and say they were looking for exactly this but couldn't leave where they were. I remember one pastor who'd driven all morning from his home in Eastern Washington. He sat in the back, tears in his eyes, just taking it all in.

We were bearing witness to what still flickered. It was a suicide mission, for sure. But it still felt holy, and it still felt worth it.

I'll return to my story in Part 3; but first, I want to explore some of the key ideas we were wrestling with in that season. Not as answers, but as honest attempts to hold space and remain faithful to what is true. I hope something in it is useful to you—that it lets you wrestle with your gods and inspires you to face your unknowing with courage. To still show up. To live in love and virtue anyway.

There's a quote often attributed to Guru Nanak that says, "Before becoming a Muslim, a Hindu, a Sikh or a Christian, let's become a human first."

In retrospect, that feels like the secret we were stumbling toward all along. The spiritual task is less about getting the answers right and more about becoming more fully human. It's the daily, difficult work of becoming someone who can live with depth and kindness; someone who can love without needing certainty.

I think that is what faith is really about. Not allegiance to a system, but the courage to kiss it goodbye while still carrying forward its deepest invitation.

So let me invite you, as we explore these next eight topics, to keep growing, to keep asking, to keep listening. Because in so doing, we are choosing a kind of faithfulness that could actually transform us into a beneficial presence on this earth.

CHAPTER 13
GOD—A WORD TOO HEAVY TO HOLD

"God would have us know that we must live as people who manage our lives without God. The God who lets us live in the world without the working hypothesis of God is the God before whom we stand continually."
— Dietrich Bonhoeffer, Letters and Papers from Prison

"The ultimate and highest leave-taking is leaving God for God."
— Meister Eckhart

After the Hoffman Process, when I let myself grieve the God I had once worshipped, things got easier. It wasn't that I stopped caring about God. I just couldn't keep pretending the old version made any sense. The question was less about whether God was real and more about whether the word itself was still worth holding on to.

In other words, I didn't lose God. I lost the illusion that I'd ever known what the word meant.

For a long time, I was certain. The Bible said what it meant and meant what it said. And God—*He*, because of course God is male, and of course He deserves capitalized pronouns—was the Author. A cosmic CEO, intimately involved, deeply personal, yet curiously bureaucratic. You obeyed or you burned. You prayed, and maybe you got your parking spot, and maybe your test results came back benign. You praised Him on Sunday and called Him Father like He was just a really good version of your dad—omnipotent and emotionally consistent.

But hairline fractures were forming. Not all at once, but like a slow thaw in spring. My friend Bart Campolo talks about his faith dying the death of a thousand paper cuts. That's it right there.

A question here, a doubt there. A child's casket lowered in the rain. A genocidal verse explained away. A prayer met with silence.

Eventually I started reading the Bible not as an oracle but as the complex ancient library that it is. Not Holy Scripture dictated by God, but penned by very human people across vast swaths of time who were trying their best to name the mystery.

And as I said before, that's when things picked up steam. I was slippery-sloping.

If this wasn't a perfect book, then maybe my understanding of the Author wasn't perfect either. And if that Author wasn't exactly who I thought it was, then maybe we never really had the relationship I hoped. Maybe it was one-sided, like talking to an imaginary friend and mistaking your own echoes for someone else's voice.

I don't say that with cynicism. I say it with reverence. With sorrow. With a strange relief. Because something about letting that image die—sky daddy, divine micromanager, capricious wish-granter—made room for something more honest. More human. More real. Something that might have enough room to hold a definition of God that still made some sense.

I found myself haunted by the mystics, such as Julian of Norwich, Meister Eckhart, and John of the Cross. They didn't seem all that concerned with literalism. They wrote of God in metaphors, in contradictions, as absence as much as presence. They seemed less interested in control and more in surrender. Less about finding God; more about being found by love.

Jean Gebser's work began to help me, too. When he wrote about structures of consciousness evolving over time—not in a straight line but in waves—I felt like he'd been eavesdropping on my last decade. He said the way we see and speak about God says more about our level of awareness than it does about God. And maybe what we call God is not a being but Being itself. Maybe God is not a noun but a verb. Not out there but through and within.

Late nights with friends like Peter Rollins nudged me further. He dared to ask: What if God isn't the solution to our anxiety, but the name we give to our deepest encounter with it? What if faith begins not where certainty ends, but where it dies altogether?

Somewhere in the swirl, I found thinkers who spoke of God as evolution's arrow, as love and complexity pulling us forward.

Then Bruce Sanguin picked up that thread, helping me see divinity not as a static ruler, but as the very impulse toward wholeness.

Ilia Delio added to it, suggesting God isn't a being *out there* but the lure of what's trying to emerge.

Process theology, too, helped open me. Instead of an all-controlling deity, God is the One who suffers with us, who lures creation forward, who changes and responds in relationship. Not omnipotent in the old sense, but infinitely powerful in love.

I started to see God less like a being and more like a current—a story, a pulse, a gravitational pull toward meaning. Everyone seemed to be pointing in that direction, from different angles.

Cosmologists like Brian Swimme write of the universe as a sacred story still being told.

Philosopher-orator of the psychedelic movement, Terence McKenna, with his wild brilliance, suggested the divine isn't behind us in some Edenic past, but ahead of us, pulling us toward novelty, complexity, and transformation.

Or the great Barry Taylor's genius: "*God* is the blanket we throw over the mystery to give it shape." Maybe one of the best one-liners ever.

Because mystery remains, even when our gods die. And maybe the best we can do is name the mystery with humility and poetry instead of certainty and control.

What fascinates me is how nearly every culture and tradition has its own name for this experience of transcendence, for this source of life, energy, and meaning that resists containment. Source, Elohim, Spirit, Christ, Tao, Brahman, the Ground of Being, the Sacred Mind, the Implicate Order, the Singularity—all of them reaching for what refuses to be pinned down.

That language made more sense to me than the image of a God who intervenes to help you pledge your favorite sorority but apparently takes a raincheck on Auschwitz. A God who helps you find your car keys but seems silent as 800,000 children die each year of diarrhea. That God—the interventionist patriarch, the magical problem-solver—had to go.

Along with the concept of God, there is the devil. Or rather, the psychological fracture caused by believing in one.

When I believed in Satan as a literal being—God's archenemy, whispering temptations into our minds—it let me bypass full responsibility for my darker impulses. Sure, I was an imperfect sinner. But also that red suited "enemy of my soul" was working overtime to take me down.

Greed? The devil.
Doubt? The devil.
Anger, fear, envy, laziness?
The devil, the devil, the devil, the devil.

This is a classic example of psychological projection: the parts of ourselves we can't accept—our fears, desires, flaws—get cast outward onto an external enemy. It's also scapegoating in action, a way to preserve perceived purity and goodness by blaming "the other." Christianity, like many traditions, uses the devil and sinners as these objects to project our shadow onto, so we don't have to face what's uncomfortable inside.

But eventually I realized that what I'd called the devil was actually me. Or at least a disowned part of me—my shadow, my unmetabolized pain, my unmet needs. Projecting it onto some cosmic villain made it easier to disown, but it didn't make it go away. It just kept it lurking in the dark, fragmented and unresolved.

Maybe that old story about the devil wasn't really about temptation. Maybe it was about our fear of our own wildness.

It's revealing that artistic depictions of the devil tend to bear a striking resemblance to a certain horned and goat-legged forest god. Somewhere along the way, the instincts that tethered us to the earth—our sensuality, curiosity, vitality—were cast as threats to holiness. The old forest god, Pan, once a symbol of earthy joy, was turned into the devil himself—a warning against the body and the natural world. When the sacred was lifted skyward, the body became suspect, and our animal life was treated like sin.

But what we exile as "evil" doesn't disappear. It waits underground for our willingness to welcome it home. To reclaim what was called the devil is to reclaim our own aliveness—the part of us that real spirituality invites us to integrate, not fear.

If there is evil in the world—and I believe there is—it's not wearing horns and holding a pitchfork. It's wearing my face when I refuse to see my own capacity for harm.

Healing doesn't come from casting out demons.
It comes from integrating the parts of ourselves we've tried to exile.
That's inner work. That's real spirituality.

So no, I don't believe in God or the devil anymore, at least not like I used to. And yet, at times I struggle with the idea that we are alone. That an infinitely powerful good guy and a somewhat less powerful bad guy aren't yanking and pulling on us in some epic tug-of-war for our souls.

Because I want there to be Something. I do. Something big enough to make sense of the ache. Something loving enough to trust. Something beyond our tribal gods and denominational rulebooks. But I wonder if the word "God" is just too freighted now. Too many wars, too many manipulations, too many broken promises wrapped in divine language.

I remember my friend Doug Pagitt, after listening to me vent my frustration about not knowing what to do with the word "God," gently saying that it helped when he stopped thinking of God as a "single sep-arate subject." That reframe widened the aperture of my mind. What if divinity isn't an external object of worship, but the field in which all things arise?

Sometimes I catch myself doing something like praying, and I don't know who I'm talking to. Sometimes I cry, and something in me still calls it holy. Sometimes I look at a tree and feel more reverence than I ever did in a church.

Atheism, I came to realize, is literally just non-theism—a rejection of theistic gods. That's where I landed too, at least for a while. But reject-ing theism doesn't exhaust the conversation. It just clears the floor. There are so many other ways to describe the Absolute.

Maybe I'll never get the word back. Maybe I don't need to.
I still can't say I know.
That's the most honest faith I've had yet.

Not-knowing. Still longing. Still listening.
Still wondering if the word is worth the baggage it's dragging behind it.

CHAPTER 14

JESUS, GANDALF, AND ME

"Myth is not a lie. It is a way of telling the truth."
— C.S. Lewis

Letting go of biblical literalism helped me meet Jesus in a new way.

For years, Jesus felt less like a living presence and more like a theological figurehead—a symbolic centerpiece for a system more interested in control than change. I felt bad for him, honestly. He'd been conscripted into a convoluted formula: a divine loophole in a cosmic legal drama, engineered by a God too holy to look at sin, yet willing to torture his own son to make peace with himself... *Um, thank you?*

I tried to make that story work. I really did. But it always felt like theological tax code—penal, arbitrary, and strangely transactional.

What changed for me wasn't only intellectual. It was both emotional and existential. I stopped needing Jesus to be a historical fact, and I started letting him be a sacred archetype. A mythopoetic doorway into the deepest truths about love, power, and humanity.

And before someone misunderstands: no, I don't mean myth as in "false." I mean myth in the older, truer sense—a story that doesn't need to have happened to be happening. A story that holds something too profound for fact alone to carry.

Like the Bhagavad Gita, or Lord of the Rings, or Star Wars, or the story of Siddhartha. They may be stories, but they're more than fiction. They're mirrors. Maps. Echoes of the human journey. And somewhere in that mythic chorus, Jesus emerged—not just as a figure in history, but as a figure in me.

My buddy Kent Dobson puts it this way in *The Christ Symbol*: "The Christ is not a religious mascot, but a mythic doorway into the mystery of being. If you stop trying to prove him, he might actually speak."

That was the move. I no longer needed Jesus to have *lived*. I just needed him to be alive in the way that myth lives inside us.

Dobson also writes: "The power of a symbol is that it cannot be nailed down. The moment you try to make it literal, it dies. Christ is a living symbol—not a trophy for the saved, but a mirror for the soul."

Death and rebirth. Despair and renewal. Wounding and wisdom. Down into the grave and up into the garden.

The myth of Jesus just gave me language for what I'd already lived—and let me live it more fully.

That shift also freed me from one of the most overused Christian debate tricks I'd inherited: the classic "Liar, Lunatic, or Lord" trilemma. It presents itself as airtight reasoning, but it's really just a theological funnel dressed up as logic. Because those aren't the only options.

Jesus could've been a charismatic teacher with some radical ideas. A literary invention. A composite of oral traditions and evolving myth. A mystic, a revolutionary, or a deeply flawed human being whose life got mythologized. Or, like Gandalf, he could be fiction—but fiction that reveals deep truth.

Nobody debates whether Gandalf historically existed, and yet we are moved by his story. His value is in what he shows us—about wisdom, sacrifice, and the redemptive use of power. To miss that is to miss the point. The same can be true of Jesus.

What if the real power of the story is in what it invites us to become?

As I let go of the literalism, the whole world started glowing with meaning. Trees preached. Bodies became temples. Acts of compassion became communion. Enemies became mirrors to our own inner darkness.

I no longer needed Jesus to be the only son of God. Because suddenly, we all were. Sons. Daughters. Reflections of the divine spark, learning to become love.

But here's the bigger freedom: I also no longer needed Jesus…at all. Not in the old way. Not as gatekeeper. Not as savior. Not as requirement.

Jesus could take his place among the sacred lineage of mythic and historical figures who light the way—alongside Siddhartha, Lao Tzu, Pema Chödrön, Dr. Martin Luther King Jr., Ram Dass, Rabi'a Basri, and yes, even Gandalf.

Jesus doesn't have to be better than the rest. Truth, beauty, and love have never belonged to one tradition, one teacher, or one text. We've inherited wisdom from all over—from saints and scientists, mystics and novelists, friends and ancestors, sacred texts and fantasy novels alike. Truth shows up where it wants to.

In Dorothy Day:

> "I really only love God as much as I love the person I love the least."

In Thich Nhat Hanh:

"When another person makes you suffer, it is because he suffers deeply within himself....He does not need punishment; he needs help."

In Eeyore (from *Winnie-the-Pooh* by A. A. Milne):

"A little consideration, a little thought for others, makes all the difference."

In Yogananda:

"The happiness of one's own heart alone cannot satisfy the soul; one must try to include, as necessary to one's own happiness, the happiness of others."

In Pema Chödrön:

"Compassion is not a relationship between the healer and the wounded. It's a relationship between equals. Only when we know our own darkness well can we be present with the darkness of others. Compassion becomes real when we recognize our shared humanity."

In Gandalf (J.R.R. Tolkien):

"Many that live deserve death. And some that die deserve life. Can you give it to them? Then do not be too eager to deal out death in judgment."

In Martin Luther King Jr.:

"Darkness cannot drive out darkness; only light can do that. Hate cannot drive out hate; only love can do that."

In Jesus of Nazareth:

"Love your enemies. Do good to those who hate you. Blessed are the poor. The mourners. The peacemakers. The merciful. The ones who hunger for justice."

These voices harmonize. They point in the same direction—toward love. Toward justice. Toward freedom from fear.

I wasn't trying to replace Jesus *or* cling to him. I was growing up. And as I did, I found I could keep the wisdom and let go of the weight. Revere the story without freezing it in dogma. Love what was useful and leave the rest.

So no, I didn't abandon Jesus. I just stopped needing him to carry the whole thing.
I let him rest—and let myself rest too.

When I gave Jesus back his humanity, I got mine back too.
And it took both of us off the cross.

He became one of many teachers who reminded me that love is still the point.

And from there, I began again—not with belief, but with meaning. Not to follow the myth, but to let it follow me into real life.

CHAPTER 15
THE RUPTURED APPENDIX
OF RELIGION

"It is a curious irony that while the truth can set us free, the desire
to always be right is itself a slavery."
—from my journal, 2015

A few years ago, Michelle and I were on a rare kid-free vacation in Encinitas. One afternoon, we wandered into the meditation gardens at the Self-Realization Fellowship—the site where Paramahansa Yogananda wrote *Autobiography of a Yogi*. Later, I reread a line I'd scribbled from one of his books:

> Become identified not with narrow bigotry masked as wisdom, but with Christ Consciousness…with universal love, expressed in service to all.

That phrase—*universal love*—still rings. Whether you call it Christ Consciousness, Buddha Nature, Atman, loving awareness…it all points to the same truth:

We already belong to one another.

Mystics have whispered this for centuries.
But exclusivist religion keeps shouting the opposite.

That's not an accident. It's a feature. It's built into most people's theology. Saved versus unsaved. Righteous versus sinners. Loved by God versus rejected by God. Us versus them.

Because when God becomes a tyrant demanding submission and correct supernatural beliefs in order to belong, then what we're worshipping isn't divine—it's human insecurity dressed up as heavenly omnipotence. And that kind of fear tends to lash out in unpredictable and incredibly harmful ways. That kind of God doesn't love people; it loves right belief. Humans are just the medium of delivery for God's true beloved.

Exclusivism is like an infected organ. An appendix about to rupture. And if we don't cut it out, it will blow up and take us all out.

The underlying assumption of exclusivism, of course, is that *we* are right and *they* are wrong. That kind of certainty is baked into evangelical Christianity from the very start. I used to think I had all the answers. Not some of them. *All of them.* At least the ones that mattered. About God, salvation, eternity, morality—you name it. I was twenty-five, married, and leading a rapidly growing megachurch. If certainty were a drug, I was deep in the grip of an evangelical high. And like any good addict, I mistook the rush for truth.

The machine I helped build —the one I later took apart—wasn't evil. It was born of longing and love, but it also ran on fear, certainty, and performance. And I knew how to keep it running.

The thing about certainty is it's seductive. Especially when you're young, insecure, and hungry for purpose. Evangelicalism handed me a story where I was the good guy, the chosen one, part of the remnant who really understood God. Unlike those Catholics or all the deceived people of other religions. Theological certainty gave me clarity, conviction, and a script to follow.

But over time, the script started to suffocate me.

I began noticing the costs: the way it split people into insiders and outsiders. The pressure to keep performing a version of holiness that looked a lot like success. The inability to admit doubt without being seen as a threat. And the subtle (and sometimes not-so-subtle) misogyny, homophobia, and nationalism that got baptized under the banner of biblical faithfulness.

I tried to reform it from the inside. I tried to make the message more inclusive, the culture more honest. But the pressure kept growing until the seams gave way. Turns out, some systems don't bend—they break.

Somewhere in that season, I met a Hindu family in a humble home in Chennai, India. Their hospitality and peace were undeniable. So was their altar. Fifteen years earlier, I might have labeled it idolatry. Now, all I could think was: *These people don't need to convert. They're already more generous, humble, and loving than I am.*

That thought shifted my entire worldview. It was one of many moments that unraveled certainty and restored curiosity.

Another one was spreading my grandfather's ashes in the forest and realizing he was the kind of man the world needed more of—kind, gentle, authentic—even though he wasn't a "high-impact volunteer" or a small group leader, and he hadn't really observed most of the religious rituals I once taught in our membership class as essential.

Each of these moments poked holes in the old garment until it just didn't hold together anymore. There had to be a wider welcome.

Bishop Spong wrote:

> We love our primary caregivers first, and then in ever-widening cir-
> cles…to our family, tribe, nation, and eventually humanity. We pause
> in a kind of fearful anxiety at every boundary that marks a transition
> into a larger orbit. The further out we venture, the more difficult it
> becomes—for we begin to see that we must love for love's sake, not
> for our sake.

That's the work:
To keep widening the circle.
To let love grow faster than fear.

And if your religion isn't evolving into a healing presence, if it can't
widen the circle, if it prevents you from loving your neighbor—then
it isn't sacred.

It's dangerous.

A religion that's afraid to die might kill to stay alive. As Voltaire is often
quoted as saying, "Anyone who can make you believe absurdities can
make you commit atrocities."

Because the problem isn't irrelevance. It's harm. And exclusivist religion
endangers everyone.

At the end of the day, a system *is* what a system *produces*.

If your washing machine stains every piece of clothing purple,
it's not a washing machine.
It's a purple dye machine.
No matter what you call it, its function is to turn everything purple.

It's like that Jesus quote: "You will know a tree by its fruit."

So if a belief system keeps producing fear, hatred, and division, then that's what it *is*.
It is a fear, hatred, and division system.
Otherwise known as rotten fruit.
And rotten fruit goes in the trash.

Somewhere along the way, I stopped caring what people believed and started asking what their beliefs *do*.
What function do they perform?
Do they shrink or expand your sense of kinship?
Do they make you more compassionate, more human, more present?

When our church affirmed LGBTQ+ inclusion, it felt like the big move. It was bold, public, costly. But it wasn't the whole story.

The deeper shift was this: I couldn't keep participating in a system that saw anyone as outside of love.

We didn't *give* LGBTQ+ people anything.
We simply stopped pretending they weren't already okay.
Already sacred.
Already held in belonging.

That move—from conditional acceptance to unconditional belonging—broke the spine of the religion I inherited. I couldn't do it halfway anymore.

As I've already said, I wasn't angry, and I wasn't trying to fight the church. But the truth was starting to rot in me, and I would have ruptured from the inside.

We need a deeper leap.
Not just inclusion: *You can sit with us now.*
But inherent belonging: *You were always one of us.*

You already belong.
So let it go.
The pressure. The guilt. The manipulation. The shame. The competition.
You don't have to belong to a religion.
You don't even have to believe in a god.

You already belong.
You belong like a wild goose belongs to the sky.
Like the ocean belongs to the shore.
Like your breath belongs to your body.

And once you and I know that,
we can stop clinging to fear
and start living in love.

CHAPTER 16
PRAYER CHAINS
AND PANIC ROOMS

"At its best, religion offers a kind of poetry and moral aspiration.
At its worst, it demands we lie to ourselves."
—Sam Harris

It starts like this: Someone gets bad news. A diagnosis. A car crash. A baby stops breathing. And within minutes, texts start flying.

"Please pray. Get everyone you know to pray."
You forward it. You share it. You say a quick one.
You wonder if it's enough.

I used to be the one who started these. As a pastor, it was my job to "mobilize intercession," to set the spiritual gears in motion, to make sure God knew how many people were asking. There's an unspoken belief that if we can get enough prayers circulating, like spiritual retweets, the algorithm of heaven might finally pay attention.

Prayer chains were our version of divine escalation.

There's a performative layer to it, too. A way of being seen doing the right thing.
If you're on the list, you're on the team.
If you pray, you care.
If you don't…well, how could you be so heartless?

But underneath that flurry of frantic prayer lies something very human: panic.

Because sometimes prayer is the only language love has left.

When it's your child, or your partner, or your own body that's breaking down, you don't care about theology anymore. As the old, condescending saying goes, "There are no atheists in foxholes." You're just scared. You're pacing the floor. You're bargaining. You're trying to find the combination lock that will make the universe undo what's happening.

And prayer becomes the panic room.

A last-resort shelter we run to, hoping the monster outside won't kick the door in. A sealed-off, soundproof vault where we whisper our most desperate words and hope, wish, or even pretend someone on the other side is listening.

It's too simplistic, though, to suggest prayer is just delusion. Because at its core, prayer is often love in disguise. It's the only language some of us know for saying, "Please don't let them go." Even when the beliefs get messy, the longing underneath them is real. It's how we try to stay connected when everything feels out of control.

When I got my cancer diagnosis, I watched the whole system flip around on me.
Suddenly I was the one people were praying *for*.
Some sent encouraging notes.
Some shared with me what God had "told them" about my healing.
Others assured me, "We're believing for a miracle."

Part of me wanted that miracle, of course. I didn't want to die. I didn't want to leave my kids. I didn't want to stop existing. But by that point,

I no longer believed in a God who answered prayer the way I'd grown up believing.

And yet, I welcomed the prayers, not so much because I believed they'd change the outcome, but because I knew they meant someone was thinking of me and pleading, "Please don't let him go."

And that's the strange truth: the gesture matters more than the theology behind it.

But there's also a cost. When your body is failing or your world is falling apart, the pressure to *believe* can feel like another layer of stress. You're not just sick or suffering through some tragedy—now you have to manage everyone else's expectations about how faith works.

Because if the prayers "work," everyone rejoices. And if they don't, it gets real quiet. No one knows what to say except for a few empty platitudes about God's ways being higher than our ways or a passive-aggressive comment about how you need more faith.

And you're left alone with your unanswered prayers and the silence of God.

It's one of the most brutal mind games religion ever played: "If your faith is strong enough, you'll be healed, protected, provided for, and kept safe." Which means if you're not…well, you do the math.

There's a verse—I used to quote it without flinching—where Jesus says, *"According to your faith be it done unto you."*

It sounds inspiring… until your daughter dies.
Until the chemo fails.
Until the prayers pour out like buckets of water over a house that still burns to the ground.

That verse has wrecked people. It turned God into a transaction machine and the person suffering into the problem.

I've sat in rooms where parents were about to remove their child from life support. I've watched them plead with God, quote scripture, lay hands, and cry out in desperation. And when nothing happened— when the machines fell silent and the room did too—they didn't just lose their child. They lost their dignity. Because someone, somewhere, had convinced them that *if they just had enough faith*, it would've ended differently.

That's the cruelty of this belief.
First it fails, then it shames you for the failure.
It lets God off the hook and makes you the screw-up instead.

When I got cancer, some people told me that healing was "already mine," that I simply had to receive it. That all sickness is a lie, or a test, or a lesson. Or worse—that it was a gift.

I know they meant well. But I also know what it did to me.
How it made me feel like I had to manage my emotional state for the sake of survival.
That my cells were listening.
That doubt itself could doom me.

That's spiritual hostage-taking.

And it's not just organized religion that does this. New Age spiritual-ity has its own way of blaming the victim—just with better playlists. Instead of "sin," it's "low vibration." Instead of God's will, it's the uni-verse "teaching you something." Some folks even say we chose our suf-fering ahead of time—that before we were born, we picked our parents, our traumas, our diagnoses like items off a soul-growth buffet.

It's neat. Tidy. Spiritually sanitized.
And just as cruel.

Because what do you say to the grieving father? The teenager with leukemia? The woman assaulted on her walk home? That their soul needed it? That they manifested it?

That's not helpful. That's just another attempt to pin down the chaos to feel in control.

I understand the impulse. We all desire to make meaning out of chaos, to avoid randomness, to believe we're the authors of our own destiny. But sometimes the most honest, compassionate thing we can say is: *I don't know.*

And pretending we do—whether through Bible verses or soul contracts—can do more harm than good.

If you're offended by that, I'm not saying to stop believing whatever you want. Just stop confusing belief with knowledge.

As Kester Brewin writes in *After Magic*, the real task isn't to keep conjuring new spells to protect ourselves from pain—it's to let the magic die. To stay present in the unfixable, the ordinary, the here. Both religion and its more psychedelic cousins are tempted to bypass suffering with bigger visions or better beliefs. But real change begins when we stop trying to escape. When we let go of the need for cosmic guarantees.

I don't believe in that God anymore—the one who heals some people and leaves the rest to wonder what they did wrong.
I don't believe in a God who needs to be convinced to save a suffocating child.

Or one who needs to be worshiped just right.
Or quoted back his own book like a spell.

I also don't pray anymore. Not in any recognizable way. I don't think of the universe as a genie or a parent or a cosmic vending machine.

We all know when someone's choking, they don't want a prayer—they want the Heimlich. Not because they don't believe in love or hope, but because in that moment, they need action. Not performance. Not piety. Just action.

In the words of Robert Ingersoll, "The hands that help are better far than the lips that pray."

But I *do* sit with people.
I show up.
I breathe with them.
I hold their hand.
And I try not to offer promises I can't keep.

There's no magical incantation that summons the gods to do our bidding.
No hotline to heaven.
No interventionist God keeping score.
Just us. Bruised and breathing.

But I still believe in healing.
I've seen it.
Not always in the body—but in the way people learn to live again after devastation.
In the way grief carves out space for compassion.
In the way communities rise around the wounded.
In the way love keeps showing up, even when the miracle doesn't.

When no god answers, the act of reaching is so human.

Faith was never meant to be a lever.
It's more like a light.
It's the light of hope you carry with you when you're surrounded by
darkness.
A light that illuminates possibility.

The God I trust now—if you can even call it God—doesn't bargain.
Doesn't punish.
Doesn't grade us on belief.

It's something quieter. Something closer. Found not in answered
prayers, but in the hands that hold us when everything falls apart.

No more altars to soothe the gods
No more prayers to tip the odds
No more priests to stir the air
To summon HIM from over there
No more chosen tribe or clan
Cathedral, mosque, or holy land
No more fear of wrathful kings
Eternal fire for temporal things
No more sense of separation
No sacrificial reparation
Though violence brings what hatred wrought
Love will mend what law could not

—from my journal, 2016

CHAPTER 17
RESURRECTION IS NOT A RETURN

"So long as you haven't experienced this: to die and so to grow,
you are only a troubled guest on the dark earth."
—J.W. Goethe

The stars died so we could be here.

It's written in the elements of your body. The calcium in your teeth, the iron in your blood, the oxygen you breathe—these were forged in ancient stars that lived, burned bright, collapsed, and exploded in death. From that stardust, planets were born. And from those planets, life emerged.

We are not just *in* the universe. We *are* the universe, awakening to itself through this pattern of birth, death, and life-after-life.

Nature is a resurrection story told in every season. Forests burn, and wildflowers break through the ash. Rivers dry up, only to return with the rain. Compost rots, and from it, tomatoes ripen on the vine. Even breath is a death and return. Inhale. Exhale. Begin again.

Nature knows how to let go.
But as humans, we struggle.

Why, when it comes to human life—especially in our spiritual stories—do we insist on dragging corpses forward?

We keep trying to revive what needs to be released—resuscitating expired identities, beliefs, roles, systems. But resurrection is not resuscitation. There's no going back.

There comes a time in every life when what once gave us meaning begins to fall apart. A worldview, a role, a self-concept—we feel it falling. If we're honest, we recognize: This is not a problem to fix. This is a death to face.

And if we're courageous, we don't just try to patch the old thing up. We let it die. And we begin to listen for what new thing might want to rise from its grave.

I'd been taught resurrection was a doctrine to believe in.
But I think it's a pattern to practice with your whole life.

Across cultures and ages, this pattern shows up everywhere: descent into darkness, surrender, and unexpected emergence. The seed falls into the soil. The caterpillar melts inside its cocoon. The ego shatters under the weight of failure or loss or awakening. And something more spacious, more whole, more connected begins to take shape.

I don't need to believe a body walked out of a tomb to find something meaningful in that pattern. What interests me now isn't whether it happened, but what it points to: the possibility of life after ego, after collapse, after loss.

Taken as myth, not mandate, the resurrection isn't about escaping death.
It's about trusting the descent.
It's about surrendering to the collapse of identity and letting love be what carries us through the grave.

That's one vision of resurrection. Not exclusive, not supernatural—just deeply human.

I preached sixteen Easter sermons. Hope was the product, resurrection the brand. Whether I believed it or not, the show went on.

What I didn't understand then was that resurrection can't be argued into existence. It doesn't need defending.
It's something to surrender to.
And it doesn't happen under stage lights. It happens in the dark.
In the wreckage.
In the places where something essential dies and something unexpected begins to stir.

And once I let that truth sink in, I could finally stop trying to resuscitate the expired forms of my life and start listening for what wanted to be born.

This is where the work of people like Bruce Sanguin opened up a new dimension for me. He describes resurrection as the ongoing, creative unfolding of the cosmos—an evolutionary movement always inviting us into deeper expressions of love, justice, and wholeness.

As he writes in *The Way of the Wind*: "The resurrection is not a reversal of death. It's what death becomes when it is transfigured by love."

That changes everything: resurrection not as a singular, magical moment but as the engine of reality.

Brian Swimme calls this universe "a celebration of emergent creativity." He reminds us that we are not outside of it, looking in. We are that creativity in motion.

"You are a flame born out of the great fire of the universe," he writes. "You are not a static being, but a dynamic becoming."

That means resurrection is not a concept we apply to life.
It *is* life.

Instead of being spectators to some divine drama, we are the continuation of it. We are stardust rearranged into sentience, mystery unfolding into movement, spirit pressing outward through skin and breath and story.

And this process does not pause when we suffer.
In fact, it often accelerates.
The soul grows teeth in the dark.
The seed splits open underground.
Right as the old paths disappear, the wildflowers start to bloom.

This is the good news I now believe:
Resurrection is something that is happening *now*.
In the collective chaos.
In your own undoing.
In the places where the old story dies and the new one hasn't arrived yet.

I no longer need to believe in some supernatural event orchestrated by a god to prove a point or launch a religion. I'm not waiting for tombs to open or clouds to part. I've left behind the idea that history hinges on whether one body got back up. That framework, once central to my faith, now feels too small for the deeper mystery we're part of.

What's far more compelling to me is a resurrection that keeps unfolding within and around us. It's what happens when life refuses to stay buried, when loss shapes us into something truer and more whole. Not a supernatural loophole. Not a theological flex. But the slow, aching, luminous work of transformation.

Collapse and emergence are how everything evolves.
Even galaxies die and rise again.
So of course we do too.

I see it in my own life. From the most archetypal vantage point, I never really left my role in the community of life. I just had to die to all the ways I was performing it from fear, ego, and inherited expectation. The work I do today still echoes the old shape. I gather people, hold space for transformation, speak about things that matter. But the posture is different. It's no longer about saving, fixing, or proving anything. It's not a return—it's a resurrection. The same song, maybe, but in a new key. Reclaimed. Rewilded. Alive in a way it never was before.

Resurrection is the pattern echoing through everything.
The Jesus story is just one symbolic lens of a universal truth.
Resurrection is literally what the universe is *doing*. What it *is*!
It is the spirit of the eternal return—life, death, rebirth.

And the invitation is to participate in it.

So let me ask you gently:
What in you is already dying?
What story is losing its shape?
What role no longer fits?
What belief has started to decay around the edges—quietly, stubbornly, maybe even painfully—while you keep trying to breathe life back into it?

Sometimes resurrection begins with noticing the rot. It begins when we stop pretending something still works, still fits, still matters the way it used to. When we finally tell the truth about what's falling apart.

This isn't a call to fix yourself.
It's not a demand to move on.
It's an invitation to face what's fading with courage and to stay open long enough to witness what might emerge.
To stop clinging to what's already gone and make space for what's coming alive.

That is resurrection.
Not the return of what was.
The arrival of what's next.

CHAPTER 18
FROM BREAKING TO BECOMING

"It doesn't interest me if there is one God or many gods.
I want to know if you belong—or feel abandoned;
If you know despair or can see it in others."
—David Whyte, "Self Portrait"

"You do not need to know precisely what is happening,
or exactly where it is all going.
What you need is to recognize the possibilities
and challenges offered by the present moment,
and to embrace them with courage, faith, and hope."
—Thomas Merton

I once had a dream that I was holding up a massive glass hutch—absurdly huge, maybe ten stories tall. It was already shattered, its panes cracked and dangerous, towering above me like a cathedral of fragility.

Behind me was everyone. My congregation. My family. My former self. All watching. All depending on me.

There was this deep, unspoken sense that if I let go—even for a second—the whole thing would come crashing down. And I would be blamed for the collapse.

I didn't know what would be worse: dropping it and being the one who destroyed everything, or holding it longer and being crushed under its weight.

I've often wondered if the hutch was me. A massive, controlled demolition of the self, publicly witnessed.

The term "deconstruction" is often used to describe what happens when someone unpacks their belief system so much that it essentially falls apart. It means you disassemble the house of cards called religion and then examine each card to see what matters, what is real, what can still bear weight.

Of course, this word is the one those of us who have walked this path often use about *ourselves*. Friends and family who are still inside the religion we left use other, more pointed phrases: He fell away from the faith. She was deceived. They walked away from God. He loved the world too much. Her heart grew cold. They denied Christ.

At first, deconstruction felt like liberation. Like I was finally thinking for myself. And I was. Every belief I unhooked from felt like a victory. Every doctrine I dismantled felt like I was reclaiming space in my own mind. The certainties that had once boxed me in were now crumbling—and it felt like freedom.

But there was also a rush to it. A kind of righteous fire. I could now see the absurdity, the hypocrisy, the manipulation I had once preached and even enforced. And I called it out. I dismantled it. I mocked and condemned it. It was exhilarating to finally say what had been buried inside me for years.

What I didn't realize at the time was that deconstruction has its own gravitational pull. It can become its own identity. Its own performance.

Its own dogma. For a while, I mistook the end of belief for the beginning of maturity. But there's a difference between breaking a system and becoming whole.

Deconstruction is necessary. But it's not sufficient.

Along with freedom, though, there was loss. They lived in the same space—my head—like disgruntled roommates who could never get along.

Losing your faith is kind of like finally selling a car you've dumped way too much money into. (Hello, Snicklefritz, my 1967 VW camper!) You know you have to let it go—but that makes it harder. All you can think about is how much you've already spent. How much of your life has gone into keeping it running. Letting go feels like admitting it was never going to work. And that's a hard kind of truth to chew.

At times I felt like Mouth in The Goonies—standing at the bottom of the wishing well, gathering up the coins. "This was my dream, my wish. And it didn't come true. So I'm taking it back. I'm taking them all back."

But after the certainties collapsed, I found myself in a kind of existential quiet. No gods. No rules. No promises. Just me, the rawness of the world, and a lot of questions that didn't come with worship songs or sermon points.

I had escaped the cage, but I didn't yet know how to live free. I was disoriented, both spiritually and psychically. The whole framework I'd used to navigate the world was gone. And though that was good and necessary, it was also deeply unsettling.

That ache wasn't a sign I'd done it wrong. It was a sign I was standing on the threshold of something deeper.

The danger, though, is that we can attempt to fill the ache, the loss, by making deconstruction another belief system. One defined by negation rather than purpose, one whose end game is to dismantle rather than build—but a belief system nonetheless.

I didn't want to empty the throne of a theistic God only to place a new guru there or adopt some new age spiritual system that would end up doing the same thing: outsourcing my agency.

I didn't want to escape one cage only to willingly walk into another, just because it had softer language or burned sage instead of incense or simply abandoned the male god for female pronouns. I didn't want to build a new identity around being "ex-Christian" or make deconstruction my brand.

I wanted integration.

Not a new answer, but a deeper presence. Not a new theology, but a more honest life. Not a new savior, but the sacredness of being here— breathing, grieving, noticing, acting.

That meant honoring what had been good in my old world. There was love there. Community. A sense of belonging. Moments of transcendence. To grow up meant being able to see the whole thing clearly—not just the harm, but the beauty—and to stop needing to define myself in reaction to it.

I'm not done growing up. But I finally stopped outsourcing my journey.

The adult path, as I see it now, isn't built on belief. It's built on presence. It's forged in grief and shadow and humility. It's not quick or branded, and it doesn't promise certainty. But it offers something religion never really did: a way to live honestly, in integrity with myself and in relationship with reality—even when nothing feels certain.

Yes, I still ache sometimes for the simplicity of the old answers. I still carry nostalgia for Sunday mornings, for shared songs, for the deep belonging of a tight-knit community. But I don't want to go back. I want to go forward—with eyes wide open, heart exposed, and feet firmly on the ground.

Not looking for heaven. Just becoming fully human.

These days, I'm less interested in answers and more interested in awareness. I still care about truth—but now I think of truth as a living presence instead of a static proposition. I've come to believe that love really is the point. Not the soft, saccharine kind, but the fierce, unflinching kind that can sit with suffering and still choose compassion.

So what now? If we're not clinging to religion, what do we build instead?

Maybe part of what's dying isn't just religion as we knew it, but a stage of human development that once needed that kind of religion to survive. I think what humanity is being invited into now is a more mature spirituality—one that doesn't need a Zeus to micromanage our weather or a cosmic judge to keep us in line, but instead invites us to step fully into our own aliveness.

Theism was like training wheels, you might say. A myth that helped us make meaning before we had the tools to ground that meaning in experience. But now, many of us are ready to move beyond that. We're growing. Learning. Evolving.

We don't need to pray to a god to fix us from the outside anymore. We need to become aware of the sacred within us.

And we don't need more creeds—we need more courage.
More capacity to be here, now, in our trembling, flawed, glorious humanity.

And the symbols, if you still like them, can serve us, but only if we set them free.
The cross doesn't have to be a blood payment. It can be a symbol of love refusing to play by the empire's rules.
The resurrection doesn't have to be a magic trick. It can be a declaration that death never gets the final word.
Jesus doesn't have to be Lord to be a lighthouse.

Personally, I'm not sure I need the symbols, although I'm certain they'll always resonate in me in some way. But what I'm after is a new ecology, not a new theology or orthodoxy. An ecosystem of shared being, where faith is measured not by what you believe but by how you live.

So instead of gathering to worship a deity we've imagined into being, we can come together to remember who we are and what matters.
To sit in awe of existence.
To celebrate the miracle of each other.
To create sacred space not because some god needs it, but because we do.
Because in the face of mystery, it's good to have each other.

Maybe that's the church of the future. A greenhouse for the soul rather than a fortress of beliefs. A children's museum where our awe is fanned into flame rather than a DMV where the most important thing is staying in line and filling out the right forms the right way.

A place where wonder is enough.
Where love and empathy are the only creeds.
Where presence and togetherness are the only sacraments.

A place where we mark the sacred with breath. With pauses. With meals shared slowly.

With time spent grieving well, celebrating well, walking barefoot in grass, tending to aching backs and tender hearts.

With the stories we tell and retell—not to prove them, but to remember what they mean.

The future of faith, if it's going to mean anything, must be embodied. Ritual must arise from presence.

So we'll need ceremonies that bless transitions—not just the "spiritual" ones, but also the real-life ones: adoption, divorce, retirement, coming out, starting over.

We'll need language that lifts us without separating us, poetry that binds us together without tying us down.

We create sacred moments not by declaring them holy, but by noticing that they already are. What we once called worship might one day look more like:

A circle of people breathing together with intention.
A Saturday morning grief ritual.
A laughter-filled barbeque.
An intergenerational storytelling night under the stars.
A silent walk through a redwood grove.
A conversation that leaves your heart open and feeling more alive.
A group therapy session.
Or something we haven't even imagined yet.

What matters is refusing to disappear. Because if God is not a being but the very Ground of Being itself, then the whole damn thing is holy.

And as long as you arrive at love, feel free to skip any of the other tools and steps.

Life is kind of like a brand-new movie on opening night. You're there in the dark, watching it unfold for the first time, breath held, not knowing what comes next. And religion—at least how it's often practiced—is like the guy in the seat next to you whispering, "I know how this ends."

Shut up. You're ruining it.
And no, you *don't* know how it ends.
Because you're here for the first time too.

That's how it started to feel to me. Like someone else's script was being imposed on my unfolding experience. Their interpretation. Their timeline. Their rules. But I wasn't interested in spoilers—I wanted to be present for the story. My story. I wanted to feel it for myself, in real time. I wanted to sit in the beauty and tension of not knowing and discover what was sacred on my own terms.

If life is a brand-new story unfolding in real time, then the communities we build—our sacred gatherings, however they look—should help us actually watch the story. Feel it. Be present in it and for it.

Not rush to explain it or spoil it with answers.
Not whisper over the mystery with our need for control.

But sit in it together.
Cry and laugh and be changed by what we see.
Let it move us.

These communities of the future won't be built on doctrine.
They'll be built on courage.

They'll be places where people can be human together.
Where grief is welcome.
Where laughter is sacred.
Where silence isn't awkward.
And where love is the only measure of success.

CHAPTER 19
COMING HOME TO EARTH

"The miracle is not to walk on water. The miracle is to walk
on the green earth in the present moment."
—Thich Nhat Hanh

In the old story, Earth was temporary—a kind of spiritual waiting room. Beautiful in places, but ultimately disposable. The real goal, I was told, was heaven. The best life came later. This one was more of a test. A qualifying run. A cosmic audition.

We sang songs about flying away, about golden streets and distant gates, about being raptured out of here before things got too bad. And for a while, that gave me something to hold on to.

But over time, it felt like a betrayal. A quiet disconnection. A refusal to grieve what's worth grieving.

Because while we were planning our escape, the forests were burning. The oceans were rising. The bees were disappearing. And the soil beneath our feet—the very stuff that gives us life—was dying.

That's what happens when your religion is built on evacuation. You stop paying attention to what's right in front of you. Around you. Within you.

What came next was a kind of homecoming.
I lost the fantasy and began to feel.

I began to see the Earth not as scenery, not as raw material for human use, but as something sacred. Alive. Intelligent. Patient. And in pain.

And beyond abandoning my old beliefs, I grieved the harm they helped justify. I started to wonder what would happen if resurrection meant returning not to heaven, but to the soil.

There's a story we've inherited in much of Western religion that says we are separate from nature. That we're here to rule it, subdue it, steward it, like managers of someone else's creation. But that story is wearing thin.

We were never separate. We were never above. We *are* Earth, in motion. Conscious compost. Animated dirt, telling stories.

That may sound sacrilegious to some. To me, it's holy.

Because it means we don't need to wait for some otherworldly salvation. We need to remember where we come from. And live like we belong here.

Coming home to Earth isn't about hugging trees or moving to a yurt. It's about reverence. About waking up to the miracle of being in a body, on a planet, spinning in the infinite dark, alive for a few brief decades.

When I think about what that looks like, I think of my grandfather, Sherman Nordquist. He was a public school teacher, not a preacher—curious, kind, and a little silly—but he carried a kind of quiet reverence for the natural world. He moved gently through the woods, pointing out lichens on a fallen log, the pattern of light through old-growth cedar. He'd remind me to keep my eyes up, to touch the moss, to take it all in.

He taught me by the way he moved slowly down the trail that reverence isn't something you perform—it's how you walk. He showed me that paying attention is its own form of prayer, and that wonder can be its own creed.

So it begins with noticing. Touching. Listening. Tending. With hearing the call of the soil to stop treating death like failure and start treating it like fertility.

Coming home to Earth means opening ourselves to grief. Because when you fall in love with this place, you feel the ache of what's happening to it. You see the plastic in the rivers, the oil in the lungs, the climate destabilizing—and it hurts.

But that grief isn't the end of the story. It's the beginning of responsibility. It's the price of real belonging.

Bruce Sanguin writes about this, calling us to evolve beyond religious escapism and into what he names "deep incarnation"— not hovering above creation, but pulsing through it. Not pulling us away, but calling us in.

The sacred is here. And we are part of it.
Just one wild thread in a much larger weave.

True ascension leads into wholeness, into humility, into participation with the Earth that birthed us. And that very participation is where meaning arises. Meaning is the felt sense of belonging and purpose that arises from being part of the great story of Life, and choosing to live in ways that deepen connection, responsibility, and wonder.

If your worldview keeps you from facing reality, loving others, or caring for the planet, then it's dangerous.

You can't live out of alignment with reality and expect no consequences.

Call it judgment. Call it wrath.

It's just cause and effect.

You piss in your own well—you drink piss water.

The myth of separation is killing us. The illusion of dominion is collapsing. And the future is asking whether we're willing to become something else—something truer, smaller, more alive.

I think the most faithful thing we can do now is get low.

Put our hands in the soil.

Apologize.

Listen.

And begin again.

CHAPTER 20
THERE IS AN OTHER

"All real living is meeting."
— Martin Buber

I've already written about how fear-based religion taught me to love with conditions. Love as sacrifice. Love as obedience. Love with strings attached—and a God who held the scissors.

But even that version of love, distorted as it was, had a kind of practical clarity to it. You fed the hungry. You visited the sick. You gave your time and your money to help someone else. In the best cases, it got people off their asses.

So when I started peeling away the religious frame, I didn't just lose a fearful God—I lost the structure that had tethered love to action. What I bumped into next were versions of love that felt more like light shows than lifelines. Energy. Vibration. Cosmic unity. "It's all love."

Maybe. But it didn't feel like love when someone was bleeding out on the floor and the best we could offer was to "hold space." I wondered if there was something in between. A third way. A way of love that didn't require a deity or a doctrine, but also didn't escape into floaty, formless abstraction. Something rooted. Real. Earthy. Something that stayed in the room.

At one point in my post-religious search for love-that-transcends, I found myself at a workshop where the big climax was—you guessed it—eye gazing. "Look into their soul," the facilitator said. "Let your hearts merge. Don't break the gaze."

I was paired with a woman who, to be fair, seemed lovely. But within thirty seconds of forced, soul-gazing intimacy, I wasn't feeling oneness—I was fighting the urge to blink and wondering if what we were smelling was someone's "natural" deodorant.

Maybe there's something profound about sustained presence and vulnerability. Maybe I'm not quite enlightened enough. But there's a difference between deep relational attunement and what might be described as spiritual foreplay for people who are afraid of actual intimacy.

After the stare-off, you were supposed to say what you "saw" in them. She told me I had "shaman eyes" and "an aura like a falcon." I told her she reminded me of my high school English teacher. It was true—and I loved that teacher—but from the look on her face, I don't think that's what she was hoping to hear.

The point is that not every loving moment needs to be a peak experience. Some of the deepest love I've known didn't involve soul gazing or celestial metaphors. It looked more like someone picking up groceries for me when I was sick. Or asking follow-up questions about my hard day. Or telling me, lovingly, to stop spiraling and go to bed.

Love isn't always a portal. Sometimes it's just a "withness" that doesn't flinch.

After a while, I noticed something about many of the people who claimed to be the most "open-hearted" and "love-aligned." They never stuck around. They'd fall in love on day three of a tantra workshop, declare it a twin flame connection by day five, and ghost by the following moon cycle. They were great at "dropping in," but allergic to depth. For them, love was something to feel, not something to build. Ephemeral. Euphoric. Preferably during an ayahuasca ceremony in Costa Rica.

Don't get me wrong—I've had my own breakthroughs under the stars. I've cried with strangers in the woods, felt the pulse of the universe in my chest, and called it love. But that kind of connection isn't what carries you. It's not the high from a retreat or the afterglow of a heart circle.

What matters is what happens after the ceremony—when the drums stop and no one's handing you cacao. When someone pisses you off, and you don't disappear into "what they're triggering in you," but actually say, "Hey, that hurt. Can we talk?"

The kind of love I trust isn't found in the ecstatic.
It's forged in the ordinary.
In taking the call. Holding the boundary. Cleaning the damn kitchen.

It's not sexy. It's not channeling. It's not a download.
It's presence that returns. Devotion without spectacle.

The ecstatic might open the door. But the kitchen table is where it's proven.

I want to pause here, because I know some people reading this have walked from religion straight into another kind of trap. It doesn't look like a trap at first. It looks like freedom. Like someone who doesn't judge you. Who speaks in calm tones. Who says all the right things about presence and energy and sacred connection. Maybe he even cried with you during the ceremony. Maybe you felt something real—because maybe some of it was real.

But now you're months in, and you're exhausted. You're doing all the emotional labor, again. You're explaining your feelings, again. You're being told that your very real pain is just "a projection" or that your need for consistency is "attachment wounding." You keep waiting for him to show up, but he's always "in process." And if you bring it up, you're met not with abuse—nothing that obvious—but with soft, subtle blame wrapped in spiritual language.

Let me say this clearly: that's not love.
Love is not the absence of conflict.
It's the presence of care.
It doesn't bypass hard conversations.
It makes space for them.
And it sure as hell isn't something you have to keep justifying while your nervous system screams.

I've been that guy at times—detached, elusive, disguising fear as depth. And I've been with people like that, too. It's confusing. Especially if you're still untangling from a religious framework that told you to endure, to submit, to spiritualize your own neglect.

But you deserve love that is mutual. Love that's not floating above life but anchored in it. Love that can say: "I'm here. I care. Let's figure this out together."

When you've been burned by religion, it's hard enough to open your heart again. But when you've also been burned by something that looked like healing—something that spoke the language of safety and awareness and sacred connection—it gets even trickier. You start to doubt your instincts. You wonder if maybe you are too much. Maybe your longing for real presence, shared responsibility, and honesty is just old trauma talking. Maybe you're the one who needs to chill.

That's part of what makes this middle path so hard.
You're trying to walk without the guardrails of religion.
You're trying to love without falling for another illusion.
You've seen how fear warps it.
You've seen how fantasy warps it too.
And you're left trying to build something steady from the ashes of both.

It takes time. It takes discernment. And it takes people who are willing to love in ways that don't always feel spectacular—but do feel steady.

Any spirituality that wants to completely do away with separation is going to get in the way of love. Love isn't the end of separation—it's how we learn to cross it. Stop flattening everyone into a mirror of your inner child. Stop dissolving every hard conversation into "oneness."

Sure, maybe in some seventh dimension—maybe on enough LSD—we are all one. Maybe this is God in drag, pretending to be billions of separate selves for the joy of rediscovering itself. But even if that's true, it can still become just another distraction.

One of the most profound things Bruce Sanguin ever said about his own psychedelic learnings was this:
"There is an other. And I care."
That's it.

To love someone isn't to transcend their separateness.
It's to show up in it. To give a shit. To respond to the particular.

I've known ecstatic love—the kind that makes you weep under the stars. The kind that feels like revelation, like your whole body remembering something ancient. But the deepest kind I've known was Michelle handing me a puke bucket during chemo. No candles. No cosmic language. No esoteric experiences. Just a quiet kind of faithfulness. She sat beside me while I trembled. Helped me to the bathroom when I couldn't stand. Rubbed my back. Told me I was still hers—even when I was bloated, gray, and balding. She didn't transcend my suffering, or reframe it as a projection, or ask me to find the blessing in it.

She simply stayed.
It was love without performance.

Love proves itself in the mess. In the care. In the choice to stay close when everything in you wants to run.

That's what I trust now.
Not the love that lifts you out of this life,
but the kind that roots you more deeply into it.

PART 3
LIFE AFTER BELIEF

CHAPTER 21
CANCER AND CLARITY

Excerpt from my journal during chemo, May 2017:

When your own body betrays you
It is off-putting, to be sure.
Like walking in on a cheating lover
it's a first-class punch in the gut
and you wonder how you didn't see it coming.
You might try and explain it away
or point out the silver lining.
Maybe you'll paint over its behavior
with thinly veiled excuses...
"I pushed him to do it."

But once everyone else is out of sight
you'll fall on your knees and weep a bit
even if you're not sure why.
Is it because you feel violated? robbed?
or do you simply shudder
because it's been like, forever
since you've inhabited your own life like this?

And somehow you're attending your own slow-motion baptism
not of water or fire,
but of blood
and flesh
and bone.

How much do you have to hate your misaligned life to be thankful to get cancer?

The thought made me laugh. It was dark, maybe, but real.

It was early 2017. I had been holding on by a thread, exhausted from the endless debates about the Bible, about sexuality, about whether I was still "in the faith." I had been unraveling spiritually and emotionally for years, but I was still holding it together on the outside. Still leading the church. Still showing up. Still pretending I could carry the weight of everything and everyone without cost. I wasn't sleeping. I wasn't resting. I wasn't okay.

So when the doctor told me I had lymphoma, I remember thinking, *Of course.* Something deep in me already knew this wasn't sustainable.

Then the next thought: *Cancer? Oh, thank God. Now I can finally quit this job and people will understand.*

I was that tired.
That burnt out.
That done.

And that's where we started, back in chapter one. A soul running on fumes. Partly devastated by the news, but also relieved. Cancer was the beginning of a tragedy and the end of a masquerade.

And maybe that was the best gift cancer gave me—clarity. No more trying to convince anyone of anything. No more exhausting debates.

The journey I was on was mine. I had done what I felt called to do at the church, but I needed freedom now. Space. Permission to explore.

I told my friends, my family, my church. I let the leadership team know toward the beginning of treatment that I was going to step back and focus on healing—and that's what I did.

There's something holy about getting stripped bare. Something clarifying. When you're sick—really sick—there's no more time for pretending. Everything extra falls away. All the ways I'd tried to earn love, prove my worth, or hold the center of a crumbling church suddenly felt absurd.

Cancer took away my capacity to fake it. And weirdly, that was a gift.

That March, I wrote a blog titled *You Probably Have Cancer*. I hadn't been officially diagnosed at this point, but something in me already knew.

> One of the big surprises to me so far has been the realization that I'm not afraid to die. You can say that, but you may not really know if it's true for you until your doctor says "you probably have cancer"... I honestly can't say that it made me afraid of "God" or eternity or heaven or hell AT ALL. But it did make me curious. About EVERYTHING.

From there, treatment began. The side effects were brutal. I lost weight, lost my appetite, lost my strength. I was nauseated for days on end—unless I smoked a joint. Gratitude for weed. Nothing else took it away. Many days, I didn't feel like eating, moving, or even thinking.

And yet, there was a strange spaciousness in it all. No meetings. No expectations. No need to explain myself or entertain visitors with casseroles who were only there to soothe their own guilt for how they'd treated me in the past.

I didn't care anymore because I was finally empty. For the first time in my life, I wasn't useful. And oddly, that became the first place I actually felt unconditionally loved. No sermons or answers or performance. Just being. Just living.

It stunned me—how much I'd built my identity around being needed, how much I feared becoming a burden, and how liberating it was to finally let that go.

I was content in the quiet. In the solitude of it. In walks by the river alone. I declined as many visitors as I could because I didn't have the energy to manage other people's discomfort or their own fear of death. I had cancer. That was enough to carry.

Sure, people dropped off baskets of stuff. Friends came by to help with the kids or the yard or the gutters. (Thank you, Brent!) But there were also plenty who seemed to be reaching out more for their sake than mine. And I wasn't interested in playing host to their uneasiness or guilt. I needed room to heal.

I wasn't mad at anyone. A big part of that came from the inner work I'd done at the Hoffman Process a year earlier. Forgiveness and understanding had washed so much away. I was at peace with the betrayals. At peace with being misunderstood.

Michelle and I focused on each other, on our kids, on the few friends who had truly stood by us. And I mean truly.
Those friends—God, I'm grateful.
We sat around together, told each other we loved one another, laughed, cried, didn't hold back.
There was nothing left unsaid.
That's a rare gift.

During chemo, one of the songs that moved me most was "Life Won't Wait" by Ozzy Osbourne. Yes, *that* Ozzy. The guy evangelicals once swore was cooking meth in hell's basement. Back in youth group, he was the gateway drug to Dungeons & Dragons—listen too long and next thing you know, you're biting the heads off bats.

But now, lying in bed, sick and heart open, I heard him sing:

Faith to live as we should and know we're all connected...
Stay strong, stay true, be brave. It all comes down to you.

It was an invitation to here-ness.
To agency.
To interconnected love.
A true worship song—one that elevated me for my actual, present struggle.

Hands raised with Ozzy.
Choosing love.
Choosing life—now.
Turns out the Prince of Darkness had become my Prophet of Presence.

The hardest thing about my cancer was the effect it had on our kids. Dodge and Ace were pretty little, but they weren't the only ones watching. Riley was in high school. Jaeger was in junior high. And while they tried to shield us from their fear—probably distracted themselves to avoid falling into despair—we could feel the weight they were carrying. They'd already witnessed the avalanche of slander and judgment we'd endured. We tried to protect them, but they weren't immune. Even at school, they were hearing things. And now *this*?

We put on brave faces. Told them I'd be home more. That we'd have lots of family time. And we did. Even as I got thinner and weaker, I tried to get out for walks along the river. I remember how beautiful everything looked. How every little thing shimmered with magic. The mountains. The sky. The way Riley laughed. The warmth of Jaeger's hugs. The way Dodge and Ace sat close and held my hand.

Loss punches a hole in us. And the light gets in, but so does the wind. That season was filled with both. We were wide open, raw, and closer than we'd ever been.

I remember lying in bed with Michelle at one point, realizing we were staring straight into the empty eye sockets of mortality—without the old dissociative comfort of a guaranteed heavenly reunion. We just held each other and sobbed, saying,

"We're together now. I feel you now. I'm holding you now. I love you."

I'll never forget what that felt like. So fucking real. So tragic—and yet, luminous. We were present to all of it. The pain, the uncertainty.

I remember lying on the couch one night, exhausted and wrecked, and thinking, *If I survive this, I cannot go back to who I was. This will mean nothing if I don't change.* I told a few close friends, "If I don't quit after this, this job will kill me."

I faced reality. I realized I had been living someone else's life and calling it purpose.

Cancer let me see through my own eyes again. It gave me permission to finally feel all the fear, all the sadness, all the weight I had carried for years as a pastor, a husband, a father, a public figure, a seeker, a performer. It brought me to surrender.

And in that surrender, something beautiful happened. I let people carry me. I let the church run without me. I let the masks fall. I started to believe—maybe for the first time—that I was lovable even when I wasn't useful.

One afternoon while my parents were visiting, I collapsed into their arms. I curled into my mom's lap, my dad's arms around both of us, and wept. Wept at the pain, the weakness, the fear. It was ugly, unfiltered, and so very human.

There's something about loss and being out of control that clarifies what matters. And what mattered in that moment wasn't theology or leadership or being strong. It was the love between us. Parent and child. That connection—raw, aching, infinite—was as precious as it was excruciating. And I let myself be held.

Months went by. My regular chemo poisonings got worse and I got thinner, but I also got freer in so many ways. The spaciousness, the walks on the river, and all the extra time to process and get my mind settled around all I'd already put down over the last few years. It was essential. And I'm grateful for the pause of it all.

By late summer, my oncologist wanted another scan. We drove in, Michelle and I, hand in hand, repeating to each other our mantra: *We accept whatever comes our way as an opportunity for growth into love.* Our voices trembled. Hope and fear holding hands.

Then the results came in: I was clear.

We wept all over each other in the car. We tracked down all the kids, shared the news, called family. That night, friends gathered around our fire pit. It was a celebration. A victory lap. A moment we'd never forget.

I felt the pull, the responsibility, not just to share our good news, but to be honest about what I believed had *really* brought us to that moment. So I posted this on Instagram:

> PRAISES!! Praise Doctors!! And nurses and researchers and biologists and pharmacists and the Scientific Method! So thankful for the decades and even centuries of data collection and trials and brave people who gave their lives to find cures for their species. My healing is in every way a result of so much collective-learning and cooperation between human cultures!!
>
> Thanks to my own Dr Van Haelst and Dr Chen!! You DESERVE CREDIT for all you've done for me and so many others!
>
> PRAYERS! Thanks to everyone who prayed for me.
>
> Thankful for prayers from my Christian friends, my Muslim friends and Hindu and Buddhist and Jewish friends... my friends from my Raja Yoga class and my Kundalini friends, "Sat Nam!!!!" Thanks to my non-religious friends for beautiful notes, warm thoughts & shared tears... I receive it ALL as a testimony of universal love & care from my fellow humans all on their own journeys within their own traditions. We are all just walking each other home! Namaste.
>
> GRATITUDE! Not all journeys have endings like this, and I don't believe "God" specially chose to heal me while innocent children are still dying of cancer or simple malnutrition... BUT, I am still grateful for the infinite mystery of my life. I don't feel entitled to ANY of it and I plan to keep living fully and loving wastefully for as long as I can... I hope my scars and the knowledge that this could always come back can be a "thorn in my side" that blesses me with the ability to mindfully return to my mortality in a deep, transformative way.

And Michelle and I posted this, too:

> To all our friends and acquaintances who have lost a child or another loved one to cancer, some other illness, freak accident or otherwise... no matter what other people claim regarding Ryan's recent healing, there exists no God who would intervene to cure a 39 year old with decent medical insurance over the 800,000 children every year who continue to die of diarrhea. Your child/loved one was not taken to teach you something, or rejected or overlooked, or short on the right number of prayers, or lacking intrinsic value in some master plan.
>
> Life is beautiful but life is also tragic and shitty. We're so so so so sorry for your loss.
>
> —Ryan & Michelle

I wrote about this once in a blog, not long after. I said that cancer didn't just force me to face death—it forced me to face how much of my life I had been spending outside of myself. That I had, in some sense, abandoned my own soul in service of a story that no longer fit.

I wrote, "The miracle isn't that I didn't die. The miracle is that I finally stopped pretending to live." Because what cancer gave me—what all the pain and uncertainty gave me—was an invitation. To return. To come home. To my body and to my one wild and sacred life.

That's when the next season began. But before I stepped forward, I had to name the deeper layer of what cancer had revealed. The scariest part was realizing how complicit I'd been in my own undoing. Gradually. Quietly. Out of survival. Out of duty. Out of some belief that my worth was tied to being needed. I saw how I'd sacrificed myself to hold a system together that no longer held me.

It wasn't just exhaustion.
I had turned the violence inward.

So—painfully and honestly—I began to let go of what was never mine to hold. Not just a job or a building, but an identity built on trying to be everything for everyone.

We'd beaten cancer. I'd been given bonus life. I felt like I was playing with house money now, and I was determined to live like it.

CHAPTER 22
THE LONG GOODBYE

One day you finally knew
what you had to do, and began...
determined to save
the only life you could save.
—Mary Oliver, "The Journey"

My doctors had kept me alive.
But staying alive isn't the same as choosing to live.
That part was up to me.
They had saved my body—now I had to save my life.

But leaving wasn't easy. It meant disentangling my identity from the institution I helped create. It meant grieving the loss of certainty, of status, of a role that once made me feel indispensable. But it was also stepping toward something. Something freer. Truer. More aligned.

In 2018, I went on a vision fast in the desert with Animas Valley Institute. Fourteen days. Four of them in total solitude—no food, no distractions. And for the first time since the diagnosis, I didn't have to be strong for anyone. I sobbed for days. I grieved everything: my health scare, the losses in our community, friendships I'd lost, the long slow death of the role I had once cherished.

I heard something deep and undeniable: *It's not yours anymore. Let go.*

Still, it took another year. I wasn't ready.

Some part of me felt like I owed a debt for the years I'd spent propping up a toxic system. The religious trauma I participated in causing wasn't intentional, of course. I never wanted to be the guy who hurt people in the name of God. And now, as I write this book, I sure as hell don't want to be the guy who gets applause for helping them heal from it.

When I preached our inclusion announcement—the one where I said out loud that LGBTQ+ people were not just "welcome" but *fully affirmed*—I knew I couldn't skip straight to celebration. I couldn't act like we were suddenly the good guys.

Because before we said the right thing, we stayed quiet.
And silence is never neutral.

The structure had been speaking for us all along. In who was platformed, who was pitied, who was passed over. Even if I hadn't said much directly, I had let the system carry the judgment for me.

So I started with that. I named the harm. I owned my part in it.
Not to flagellate myself.
But to stop avoiding.
Avoiding the impact.
Avoiding the privilege.
Avoiding the quiet complicity that let love be conditional for far too long.

If this story has any integrity, it has to include this:
I hurt people. Even quietly. Even with good intentions. Even by waiting too long to speak.
I'm sorry.
This book is not a fix.
It's a small attempt to tell the truth of my process.
And maybe take back what I can.

Which is what I was already trying to do, long before I left. Those last few years—from 2016 to 2019—every sermon, every whispered doubt from the stage, every reframing of an old story… That was me trying to take it back. To untangle the knots I had helped tie. To walk backward through the very stories I once told with such conviction.

I remember thinking I could just leave. Quietly slip away and let someone else deal with it. But I couldn't. It felt like I had unleashed something I had to reckon with. Like a rabid dog that I either had to heal… or put down.

And in the end, I put it down.

I finally pulled the trigger in the summer of 2019. I visited some friends graduating from the Hoffman Process in California, which Michelle and I had done a few years earlier. I knew the power of that work. Being back in that space made it clear: I couldn't keep avoiding what was next.

The next morning, as I was driving to the airport, a Noah Gundersen song came on. One stanza pierced right through me:

> Despite all my reservations, I've been doin' this for years
> Hopin' that some magic touch would finally make it clear.

I pulled over and wept. I knew it was time. I was the only one still holding myself hostage.

When I got back to Seattle, I met with Peter and Kristen—my dear friends and part of my leadership team—and told them I was ready. They received it with so much grace. We cried. We hugged. And I said I needed to leave the town I'd lived in, loved in, and nearly died in. I needed sun. New energy. I needed to be "just Ryan" somewhere else.

So, with their blessing, Michelle and I resigned, and they took over leadership of the church. On January 1, 2020, we moved to Encinitas, California.

Since then, I've reckoned with the part of me that hated to stay but struggled to leave. It wasn't only about the part of me that had participated in toxic religion. I'd spent years unwinding that. This was about the part of me that kept holding the weight long after it was mine to carry—the one who felt responsible for everyone else's stability. I wanted to make sure my staff landed on their feet, that their families were cared for, that the organization itself didn't default on its debts.

But that kind of caretaking, noble as it looks, was also a form of self-abandonment. Leaving was laying down that burden at last.

I stopped trying to earn forgiveness.
And started practicing it—toward myself.
I don't excuse the ways I participated in toxic religion.
But I won't abandon the one who's still learning how to live differently.

That younger me didn't need punishment. He needed someone to stay.
To witness.
To hold.
To say: you were wrong, and I still won't leave you.

So I'm staying with myself. Not as a hero. Not as a savior. Just as a guy who's done hiding. Part of the process has been learning to face who I was with both compassion and honesty, without needing it to be tidy.

It took me a long time to see that healing isn't just about letting go of the past—it's about learning to love it, too. If I can't see the beauty in what was, then I'm not really growing, only reacting.

And from that place, this is what I'm learning to trust:

I used to stand on stages and speak for God. Now I listen from the depths. I traded certainty for curiosity, dogma for direct experience. I walked out of the church with nothing—and somehow a life emerged where truth isn't handed down from a book, but wrestled from my body, my story, my brokenness.

I've faced illness that stripped me bare. I've held my closest relationships in the fire and learned to choose evolution over escape. I didn't transcend my ego. It got beat down—publicly, repeatedly. And somehow, what remained was more real.

I'm not a spiritual authority. I'm a man who's bled in public and kept going. A man who stopped outsourcing his worth to borrowed beliefs.

If there's redemption here, it's not in getting it all right. It's in telling the truth, staying present, and loving with whatever remains after the old maps are gone.

To show that after the fire—after the humiliation, the heartbreak, the loss—something real still remains.

Not a perfected man. Certainly not a saint. Just someone still here.

A man, finally free.

<h1>CHAPTER 23
NOTHING TO PROVE</h1>

"I've already lost contact with a few people I used to be."
—Joan Didion

After leaving the church and landing in Encinitas, I didn't know what would come next. But what came first was stillness.

For the first time in years, there were no sermons to write, no systems to manage, no theological tension to navigate. Just the simplicity of a sunrise, Michelle's voice, and the hum of my own body finally slowing down. There in the Encinitas sunrise, I started noticing the songs of unfamiliar birds each morning, and I realized I'd never really listened before.

It took time to adjust. The adrenaline of leadership had been masking so much. Now, the silence felt both awkward and luxurious. I was used to measuring my worth by how much I gave, how many people showed up, how well I performed. Without those metrics, I had to learn how to simply be. Then one night, Ace fell asleep on my chest, and the enoughness of that moment felt like grace. And being wasn't passive—it was the most active thing I had ever done. To stay present in my body. To listen to my kids without formulating a teaching illustration out of it. To walk without a podcast, just to hear the rhythm of the waves. This was the slow return to myself.

Beauty started finding me in the ordinary. The way the pelicans flew down the beach, wings skimming the surface like they trusted the air would hold. The stretch of sky at dusk. The sound of my own heart-beat. I stopped needing to explain life and began to feel it.

Not because I had a new set of answers, but because I had stopped looking for any.

But something else surprised me too: the absence of what had always held me back. There had been this distracting background hum for years—a feeling that I wasn't allowed to enjoy my life. That I had to earn it through output, service, self-betterment. And when it was gone, I finally saw how much pressure I had internalized.

I remember writing, not long after we arrived in San Diego: "There was never anyone holding me back but me." It hit hard. Because it was true.

I began to enjoy the simplicity of being me.
Not proving anything.
Not fixing everything.
Just being.

Grief still came in waves—grieving the community I loved, the role I once held, the people I disappointed, the younger version of myself who tried so hard to hold it all together. But alongside that grief was a growing gratitude. I was alive. I was present to life. And that was enough.

Living awake isn't about some enlightened state. It's about returning, again and again, to presence. When I catch myself drifting into per-formance, I return to the moment. When I get lost in old narratives, I return to what's real. I remember: *Just this. Just now.*

I had moved from content to contact. I don't need to know what it all means. I only need to live like it matters. To be here and to care.

And then—almost without trying—we stumbled into a kind of community I didn't even know I needed. Or trusted.

In the middle of 2020, still raw from everything we'd let go of, we found ourselves surrounded by the most loving circle of tender spirits. Strangers at first. Then something else. Something family-adjacent. It didn't make sense. No one is that shiny—not a whole group of people who just met.

But they were. As I slowly let my heart open to them, I released pain I didn't realize I was gripping. And in that softening, I stepped into a world of connection.

I remember looking back a year later and writing:

> Michelle and I were packing up our house to move to Encinitas wondering what life would look like next. We had no idea the blessings that awaited us in these precious hearts. Whether it's a karmic soul cluster thing, or just dumb luck, massive gratitude to everything in life that drove us down the road to you.

That group of friends became something sacred to us. For once, we were just Ryan and Michelle. No microphones. No audience. No need to impress or explain. Just beloved.

Most evenings we'd watch the sunset together at the beach, talking and laughing as the sky went pink and the air cooled. Nobody ever left without hugging everyone. It felt like summer camp for grown-ups—one long, unplanned season of connection. There were group dinners and beach walks, meditation circles, impromptu bonfires, and a few Airbnb retreats to the mountains, the desert, even Yosemite. There was always something happening, but nothing we were trying to make happen. Just life spilling over, held in a web of affection and ease.

There was joy, laughter, playfulness. Our boys were wrapped in warmth and belonging, held by a community that loved them just as they were. It felt like grace. The real kind. The unearned beauty that catches you off guard. And yet, letting it in wasn't easy. In fact, it was terrifying.

I wrote in my journal that year:

> Over this last year I've had to shed some old, limiting parts of myself. But not because of pain, loss or difficulty. It was because of sweetness, love and joy. They've pig-piled me this year... but in the onslaught of all that goodness, I've had to take a hard look at the ways I've been pushing all of those things away. What the hell!?

It's one thing to ache for love and connection. It's another to let it in.

There's a kind of emotional armor that forms after enough rejection and disillusionment. It protects you. It helps you survive. But it also blocks the very thing you're hungry for.

One morning, after a meditation circle on the beach, I found myself lying in the grass during a breathwork session—sunlight on my face, something swelling in my chest. I could feel an emotion rising, but also my defenses locking it down. *Not here,* I thought. *Not around strangers.*

Then a woman named Summer—now a dear friend—placed one hand over my heart and the other gently on my jaw. I had a choice: brace or soften.

I chose to soften.
To open.
And to weep—grief and relief, tangled together.
I had made it. I was here. My pilgrimage out of the pastorate was over.

And since that moment, something's been different. I'm not done healing. I still flinch sometimes. But I've been choosing tenderness more often. Even when it scares me. Even when it costs me the old reflexes I once mistook for strength.

And yes, I'm probably more likely to get hurt now.
But I'm also more likely to live freer.
Lighter.
More beautifully.

Because life is a gift.
And I'm finally learning how to receive it.

Gratitude to that circle of wild hearts who reminded us what love feels like when it's free.

CHAPTER 24
THE MEDICINE—
PSYCHEDELICS AND
THE SACRED

"The Western Industrial civilization is the only group
in the entire human history that doesn't hold nonordinary states
in great esteem, and doesn't have any use for them,
actually has pathologized them; every other culture
has spent a lot of time and energy trying to develop
ways of inducing nonordinary states."
—Stanislav Grof

"Only those who risk going too far can possibly find out
how far one can go."
—T. S. Eliot

Let me rewind a little, to the summer of 2018. I was back from my vision quest, feeling like I knew—in my bones—that the end was near. I couldn't quite name it yet, but I had begun charting my path out of ministry.

I'd been in conversation with Bruce Sanguin for years by then, and he'd become one of my most trusted guides. In the midst of one of our long talks—as I wrestled with the reconstruction of my worldview— he mentioned psychedelics. He suggested they might offer me deeper vision, more self-compassion, and perhaps even a way forward. A path not just out, but through.

My friend Dave had already gone up to Bruce's remote Denman Island for a psilocybin journey, and he came back wide-eyed with wonder. That sealed it. Michelle and I began making plans to see what this was all about.

By that point, I'd let go of so much. Theologically. Socially. Professionally. I felt like a kid again—reborn in some strange way, rediscovering the world with no dogma to contain it. No guardrails. No divine behavior manual or invisible scorecard.

It reminded me of the final moments of *The Village*, by M. Night Shyamalan. The blind protagonist, Ivy, escapes her isolated religious community by climbing over a wall that, until now, she hasn't even known was there. She believes she's venturing into a dangerous unknown, but what she finds instead is the modern world. The community that she thinks has been protecting her has actually been keeping her hostage.

That's how life felt for me in that season—post-religion and pre-everything. I was exploring; I was journeying. And I was ready to discover what lay beyond the wall.

Soon after that, I found myself in a wild cabin in the woods. Owls everywhere. Which blew me away, because I'd been having powerful dreams about owls for years—dreams that stirred something deep in me. And not only dreams—*real* owls had been showing up in my waking life, too. One had scared the shit out of me a week earlier, flying straight at my head and screeching, then landing in the tree beside my house to stare directly at me.

And now, here I was, with a handful of dried mushrooms in my palm, about to take a leap into... I didn't know what.

I sat down to chew them up and looked across the tiny room, only to find myself staring directly into the eyes of a huge owl painting.

Sheesh, I thought. *Okay. Let's not get all weird. I haven't even taken anything yet.*

A few minutes later, I was gagging on the next handful of mushrooms, thinking, *If I puke this up, I'm going to have to eat my puke.* Thankfully, I powered it down. Dry and awful, but down.

Bruce was on his way over, and I'd just have to wait for him as I let this come on.

I could feel my heart pounding. My breath was a little short. I stepped outside to get some air and sat in the sunny, grassy clearing near the cabin.

Pretty soon, everything went still.
My mind relaxed.
My body softened.
And tears came to my eyes.

Oh my god…
I could never have imagined.

The grass and the trees were aware of me. They welcomed me to this place.
Okay, *now* it was getting weird.
But I didn't care.

I laughed at how much money people spend on beach vacations—flying across the world just to scroll Instagram poolside—and here

I was, more present, more at peace, more connected, than I'd ever been in my life. No ocean view. No playlist. Just grass. Trees. Birds. Awareness.

Bruce arrived not long after, and I could feel his gentle, loving presence the moment he stepped into the clearing. Gratitude for his role in my life washed over me in waves.

That first journey was a hinge that swung open a whole new chapter of my life.

I remember telling Bruce: "In one hour, these mushrooms gave me everything religion promised me my whole life but never delivered."

There was a radical awareness of sacred presence—near me, around me, within me—*as* me.
A unity of conscious awareness that felt playful and silly, childlike but also wise.
I couldn't tell the difference between what I might describe as "unconditional love" and "me."
And I didn't care.
It didn't matter.

I was home.
I belonged here.
And life had brought me to this moment at just the right time.

Insights and epiphanies streamed through me.
Moments of grief, clarity, forgiveness.
Inner resolution to old pains.
Fresh ways of seeing events I'd clung to for decades.
I saw my parents with new eyes.
I saw myself with kindness.

There were visions about my purpose. What my "soul" wanted. Which was funny, because at that point, I didn't even believe in a soul. But the medicine, I've noticed, isn't particularly concerned with beliefs.

It would take too long—and honestly, it would probably get boring— to describe everything that happened in that first journey. Trip reports can be tedious to read. But I had opened a door in consciousness and stepped into a vast, interior terrain that I would eagerly and deeply explore over the next two years of my life.

Everyone responds to their first psychedelic experience differently. For me, there was no going back. I was determined to follow the thread, to see how deep the rabbit hole really went.

Michelle went next. She traveled with a dear friend, and they took turns spending a day each at the owl cabin, launching into the depths.

Our curiosity was piqued—and from there, we dove in. We began pursuing every kind of psychedelic compound we could find.

And, per usual, I started collecting a research library. Books on the pharmacology of each substance. The history of entheogens. The cultures and traditions that had held these medicines for centuries. I wanted to understand what I was getting into. I wanted to know the map—or at least the history of those who'd walked similar paths.

Looking back now, I honestly think we did way too many drugs, too fast, with too little integration. But we were green. Naive. And so ridiculously excited. We had glimpsed the edge of some vast Mystery, and we wanted more.

Drugs weren't really a part of my life for most of my adulthood. Sure, I'd done some mushrooms in high school, and I definitely had some fun times smoking joints with my buddy Alec while listening to A Tribe Called Quest in his old Subaru in the woods. But no one would've called me a stoner.

It wasn't until Washington State legalized marijuana in 2012 that it entered my life again. As soon as the law passed, our staff meeting erupted with the question: "Can we smoke weed now? It's legal."

We weren't exactly the church of moralism. We already had a liquor license and a keg in the kitchen. We were known for taking liberal stances on social issues, and this felt like just one more thing. I shrugged and said, "Sure. Just don't be an idiot."

Which, incidentally, was *literally* in our staff handbook.

"Don't be an idiot" simply meant to use discernment. Don't undermine your own leadership. Be safe. Be dependable. That had worked for alcohol. I figured it would work for weed, too.

What I didn't realize then was how important cannabis would become for me in the years that followed—especially when everything hit the fan.

During the backlash around LGBTQ+ inclusion, I was smoking enough weed to make Snoop Dogg pass out. It was the only way I could shut my brain off after getting yelled at in a gas station or reading another furious email accusing me of being a "closeted homosexual."

I'm also deeply thankful for marijuana during my cancer journey. The anti-nausea pills were a joke, and the only two things that brought real relief were highly potent Rick Simpson oil and—my personal preference—a good, old-fashioned Bob Marley joint.

I don't smoke anymore. The interest completely left me almost as soon as I started using psychedelics. I just haven't wanted it.

No judgment to those who do, though. Most of the people I know who "maybe smoke way too much weed" are super nice and fun to hang out with. I'd much rather end up in a dark alley with a stoner than a drunk.

But psychedelics showed me something: I'd been using alcohol and weed as coping mechanisms. To numb pain. To survive exhaustion. And once I started taking psychedelics—which were getting me in touch with the very things I was running from—I didn't need the buffer anymore.

I didn't need to escape. I needed to feel.
And then, I needed to heal.

By mid-2019, we were pretty deep into our exploration of LSD and the classic psychedelics. After two ayahuasca ceremonies, we spent months integrating what we'd seen—as individuals, as a couple, and with our little crew of fellow psychonauts.

I probably would've called myself a happy atheist at that point. Or something close. I was convinced love was real, and I figured that if the universe turned out to be meaningless, so be it. Love made enough meaning of its own.

Then a friend invited me to try 5-MeO-DMT.

Some people call it "toad." What I was offered was a synthetic version—jaguar medicine. You vape it out of a glass cylinder. The entire experience lasts maybe 10 to 30 minutes.

This isn't a book about describing drugs or the neuroscience behind how they work. But that trip? That one *launched* me.

Launched me out of this universe and into an experience I could only describe as…GOD.
Not some bearded overseer or a hallucinated deity—but everything dissolving into one boundless presence of loving awareness.

Now isn't that obnoxious?

After everything I've said about deconstructing religion and leaving belief systems behind, suddenly I do some drugs and I'm back to God?

Not so fast. I'm still not sure what that was. Maybe it was just brain chemistry—the right molecule meeting the right receptor and triggering a supernova in my neural net. Maybe it was all inside me. Or maybe—just maybe—I encountered something real. Something…out there. Or in here.

I honestly don't know. But that experience rocked my world.

I have never—*never*—felt more certain of anything than I did in those moments:
That *all is love.*
That there is an endless ocean of love running through me, to me, and as me.
That I come from this love.
That I will return to this love when I die.
And that there is absolutely nothing to fear.

Is that true?

Jesus, I don't know.

But I've never felt something so true.

That experience shifted me.
From optimistic atheist to "I think we're gonna be okay."

After a full twelve months of exploration, I started noticing deep changes.

I was kinder. Slower. Gentler.
More present with my kids.
Less reactive. More spacious.

I didn't get triggered anymore when someone at the grocery store tried to corner me about the Bible. I could finally see them—not as adversaries, but as people. People who were afraid. And I could stay grounded. I could be loving.

The medicine was helping me see Michelle in a new way, too.

She's always been my best friend. And we've always had an electric sexual connection. But this was something different. Something in our bodies was uncoiling. It felt raw and primal and powerful—and it was undoing a lot of repression we hadn't even known we were carrying.

It felt like being reborn.
Like seeing each other—and ourselves—with new eyes.

We were both coming more alive.
To our senses.
To our values.
To our friendships.
To our bodies.
To our lives.

I don't want to make all this sound easy. Many of the journeys were hard. Some were agonizing. Full of pain, grief, and emotional upheaval. But that's exactly what made them so healing.

Unlike most drugs in a psychiatrist's office, these weren't numbing our pain.
They took us directly into it.
Helped us face it, feel it, reframe it, forgive it, bring compassion to it—and let it go in trust and love.

It was also revealing—almost hilariously so—how much of life is a series of ridiculous agreements to societal structures that make no real sense.

That's part of what made it so obvious why these substances are illegal. LSD and drugs like it might dazzle you with color, but they also show you things. Things about power. Authority. Control. They reveal how manipulation sits quietly at the center of so much of what we call society—and certainly religion.

We weren't just tripping. We were deconstructing assumptions baked into the very fabric of our culture. We were letting go. Letting go of the pressure to fit in. Letting go of the need to see the world like "normal" people do.

As I sit here eight years later, looking back on all the work, the pain, the ecstasy, and the experiences of what I can only call Divine Union, I am in awe of all that these compounds have offered me. I'm not advocating this as prescriptive for anyone else. To be sure, there are risks, and dallying around uninformed and naïve with any kind of drug is dangerous. Psychedelics can make some people worse, not better.

But for all the moments my eyes have been opened, for all the times forgiveness rolled to me and through me, for all the sweet exchanges

I've had with the love I encountered at the center of myself and this mysterious universe, I am eternally grateful. These tools have brought me closer to my heart and all my imperfections and offered me back to the world with a grounded sense that love really is the power and healer of everything.

I didn't substitute chasing an elusive god for an escapist's high. These drugs have always refocused me on this world and this life in a way that affirms it all and energizes me with loving compassion toward myself first and then to all of life. And in that I am forever and always changed.

Looking back, I see how every journey—no matter how wild—was guiding me home. At its best, sacred medicine doesn't send us away from the world. It brings us back—clearer, softer, more in love with being alive. It reminds us that divinity was never elsewhere; it was here all along, pulsing through the ordinary.

CHAPTER 25
THE SHAPE LOVE TOOK

"Praise be to love where there is no possessor or possessed,
but the two are delivered."
—Jorge Luis Borges

As we explored new ways of healing, thinking, and existing, it was only natural that more questions would follow.

One of the biggest was about marriage itself.

What follows is my side of that story—our story, really—but told through my eyes. Michelle's experience is her own, and while we've shaped this chapter together over many conversations, I can only speak from where I stand.

Now that we no longer believed in gods or institutions to define it, what did our partnership mean? What held it together if not theology, gender scripts, or tradition?

For years, marriage had been framed as a sacred covenant—a reflection of God's unchanging love. There's something beautiful in that metaphor. But once we let go of the theological scaffolding, we had to ask: What holds it now?

What we found wasn't loyalty to an institution, but loyalty to each other's becoming. It was about staying with what was real, even when it changed shape, even when it stretched us.

It's one thing to say you're committed to love, but another to actually practice it—to keep showing up, to stay curious, to listen to who your partner is today, not just who they were when you first met.

We've learned that presence in a long-term partnership doesn't mean we never change. It means something steadier:
I'm here.
You and I are good.
Our bond is real.
I'm not going anywhere.
And I want to keep knowing you.

But before we could explore what partnership really meant, we had to become individuals again.

We met as teenagers—wide-eyed, idealistic, and swimming in the waters of church culture. When you fall in love that young, you often build a life together before you fully build a self. So the first part of our journey was catching up to who we were becoming.

Our respective paths—especially through healing and self-inquiry—gradually unraveled some of the inherited roles we'd accepted without question. Religious frameworks, gender expectations, even subtle assumptions about what marriage is supposed to look like—all of it came up for review.

I remember looking at Michelle across the kitchen one night and asking, half-smiling, "So does this mean we're not each other's accountability partners anymore?" That's the church term for keeping tabs on each other's holiness.

The ambiguity itself was part of the work: learning to sit in the tension, to recognize what no longer fit, even before we knew what might replace it. From that ground of slow, uncomfortable individuation, our partnership began to evolve. Instead of a fixed shape to protect, it became a living thing we had to keep listening to. Attentiveness became our promise.

We began to see love as a conversation, not a contract. As a practice, not a possession. We stopped trying to fit into other people's definitions and started asking better questions of our own.

What kind of partnership brings out our wholeness?
What does commitment look like when it's rooted in freedom rather than fear?
How do we keep choosing each other with open eyes, not obligation?

The more we asked, the more we realized that what sustained us wasn't sameness but honesty.
Truth became our north star.
Even when it was inconvenient.
Especially when it was inconvenient.

We both had to learn how to tell the truth and stay. To hear it and not collapse. To keep finding each other in the space between who we'd been and who we were becoming. Sometimes honesty left us quiet for hours, sitting side by side on the couch, hands still touching but hearts pounding.

We started naming our needs and desires more honestly—not as demands, but as invitations. The mountain of fear I had to overcome to speak that honestly was immense. Early attempts at this kind of honesty were awkward. But even awkward honesty was better than polite distance. We learned that when we could speak freely and stay connected, something sacred happened. More of each of us could be visible, and that visibility brought us closer.

That process revealed what partnership means to us now: a practice of truth, freedom, and care.
It's not about guarding a structure; it's about nurturing a living bond.
It's not about safety through control, but safety through trust.
And trust, we've learned, still trembles sometimes.

Over time, we realized how much of what we'd believed about marriage wasn't divine at all—it was cultural. We'd inherited a set of unspoken rules about gender, roles, and desire, and we'd been told they were universal. But they were just local customs dressed up as cosmic law.

What a relief to see that.
It meant no one owns love.
It meant we were free to define it ourselves.

Everywhere we looked, the boundaries and expectations shifted with time and place. What one culture calls sacred, another might call strange. That realization didn't make love less meaningful—it made it more miraculous. Because it meant there was no single template. Just an endless diversity of ways to live connection.

So we began asking: if every culture writes its own script, what kind of story do we want to live inside? One built on fear and control—or one rooted in honesty and trust?

Instead of relying on religion or tradition to define us, we learned to ask simpler questions:
Is this kind?
Is this conscious?
Is this aligned with what matters most?

And what we found surprised us. The more freedom we gave each other to be whole, the more drawn to each other we became. It turns out that love, when it's not trapped by performance, has a way of renewing itself. It still catches me off guard sometimes—how telling the truth makes her eyes light up, how vulnerable disclosure can feel like a shot of adrenaline, how honesty can feel like foreplay.

The most erotic thing, it turns out, is honesty. Being known and seen again without being managed. The thrill now is in being met as a whole person, not discovered as someone's missing piece.

We also came to see how modern relationships often ask one bond to do what whole communities once did—to hold stability, friendship, passion, purpose, and belonging all at once. There were long seasons of our marriage when it felt like we were carrying every role in the village between us, expecting the other person to meet all our needs, to be our entire universe. Being someone else's "everything" sounds romantic at first, but it doesn't actually work in real life. It leads to control, to possessiveness, to codependency. It stifles intimacy and suffocates the romance it promises to create.

We realized that intimacy doesn't thrive under control.
It lives in curiosity.
In mystery.
In the space between two sovereign selves who keep choosing each other.

Sure, there was a time when rules made us feel safe. And some of those rules did protect us, at least for a while. But eventually, they started to feel like scaffolding we'd outgrown.

The kind of love we wanted couldn't be scripted or controlled. It needed honesty. It needed space. And it needed discernment—the slow, grown-up work of asking:
What's most ethical here?
What honors both of us?
What builds trust, not just between us, but within us?

We don't know exactly how our relationship might evolve over time, and that's okay. We're not trying to lock things down. We're trying to stay conscious. To stay real. To keep choosing each other—not because we're supposed to, but because we still want to.

Along the way, love asked us to expand in ways we couldn't have imagined. There were seasons that stretched every definition we'd inherited. There were moments that required courage, truth, and a deep trust in each other's goodness. More than once, expansion felt like being broken open. We had to learn that the breaking, like a seed splitting, was part of our growth.

We learned that love and honesty aren't opposites, and that the most sacred commitments are the ones that keep evolving.

There's a song by Sabrina Claudio called "Before It's Too Late." It's haunting and gorgeous—one of those songs that feels like it's whispering right into your ribs. It's about capturing ecstasy while we're still alive. About not wasting the moment. Every time I hear it, I'm taken back to a summer evening with friends at a mountain cabin in Oregon. The golden hour. The air soft and warm, everything lit up with that impossible kind of beauty.

Michelle was sitting on the deck, hair blowing wildly in the wind. She wasn't posing—just present. Unguarded. A woman who had lived, and wept, and mothered, and risked, and endured, and loved through fire. She looked like freedom.

I caught her eyes and felt everything we'd ever been crash through me at once. The years. The grief. The forgiveness. The sex. The therapy. The kids. The fights. The growth. The ways we'd rebuilt marriage in our own language. The stupid inside jokes. The secret language shared only by people who've been together more than half their lives.

It leveled me in the most devastatingly beautiful way—like love had become too big for my body. And Sabrina kept singing:

Let me adore you now
Before it's too late.

That moment felt like everything love could be.

But it wasn't new. We'd been building that kind of love since the beginning.

We got married on September 19, 1998, in a church filled with people and pipe organs and tradition. And I'm grateful for that day. But it's not the anniversary we celebrate anymore.

The real one came earlier—April 1, 1996. We were sixteen and seventeen, still kids. There was plenty of God in our lives back then, but that night wasn't about beliefs or roles or scripts. It was just us, walking through the rain, holding hands, nervous and giddy and fully alive. Then that first kiss.
Damn.
Like the world rearranged itself around a new center of gravity.

That was the moment—before the church got involved, before the government signed off, before we cared what anyone else thought. That was when it all began.

No one officiated it. But we didn't need them to. That night mattered because it was real and it was ours.

There's so much more I could say about what our love has become—enough for another book, maybe. But this is the heart of it: our love didn't need a structure when it started, and it doesn't need one now.

We know who we are.
We take responsibility for what we want.
And we keep leaving room for each other's continued evolution.

That's the kind of love we were returning to all along.
Before the rules.
Before the frameworks.
Just us.

We keep meeting each other.
And falling in love again.

CHAPTER 26
STILL FAMILY

"One cannot be human by oneself. There is no selfhood where
there is no community. We do not relate to others as the persons
we are; we are who we are in relating to others."
—James Carse

Love kept widening its circle.

First between us, then—slowly—back toward the families we came from.
After everything that had changed, staying connected to them became
its own kind of practice: truth and tenderness over agreement.

We never had "the big fight" with our families. There was no slammed
door, no dramatic confrontation, no fiery debate about what we
believed or didn't anymore. But everything had shifted. Quietly. Heav-
ily. Without anyone needing to say it.

When I left the faith I was raised in, I lost a shared vocabulary with the
people who had loved me the longest. And instead of screaming and
kicking, the loss whispered. It echoed in the silences.

Sometimes it was just a look. Or a question they were afraid to ask.
Or that soft "we're praying for you" that landed somewhere between
concern and caution.

I didn't blame them.
But there was grief in that gap—this subtle ache around the people
who had shaped me.

And still... we stayed. All of us.

There's something to be said for that.
We kept sitting at the same table.
Kept laughing at old stories.
Kept showing up at holidays and birthdays and dinners that didn't require shared theology to be meaningful.

It was love.
Not the kind that demands agreement.
The kind that remembers how to listen.
The kind that knows when to let something slide because the relationship matters more than the conclusion.

Michelle's parents are committed Christians. So are mine. But it's more than that. My parents were pastors. Their lives were stitched into the same church fabric mine had been. And when I walked away—publicly, painfully—I know it created ripples I may never fully understand.

People asked them questions. Tried to argue with me through them. I'm sure they wanted my family to speak for me, or against me, or just to explain me.

And I've wondered many times what it must have felt like for them to watch the story unfold from a distance. To see me become someone they maybe didn't recognize.

One of the hardest things for me was losing that feeling of knowing I made them proud.
There's nothing like that feeling when it's there.
And nothing like that ache when it's not.

A few years ago, I invited my dad to take a road trip with me. Just the two of us. Through Oregon, his home state. I wanted to see the places he grew up, the town he was born in, the churches he stumbled into, the one where he met my mom, the one they left to plant the church I grew up in. It felt like a pilgrimage. Into his life. Into mine.

I had an unspoken hope that we could meet again. Man to man. No pulpit. No pressure. Just... us. I didn't want to convince him of anything. I wanted to say I was sorry.

Sorry for the pain.
Sorry for the distance.
Sorry that my journey—however honest it's been—put him in the crosshairs.

We were driving through his old neighborhood when I finally got the courage to say it.

"I'm sorry I'm not in the faith anymore. I'm sorry if I've made things harder for you."

He didn't miss a beat. He put his hand on my shoulder and said, "I've always been proud of you. That's all I'll ever be. You don't have to be anything other than Ryan—ever."

I'm crying just writing this.
Because I didn't know I needed it so badly.
But I did.
And he knew.

That trip—those conversations—were healing in ways I can't measure. We didn't magically see eye to eye on everything. But we saw *each other*. And that was enough.

On another trip to San Diego, right after my vision fast, with my heart scraped clean and tender, I asked my parents to go on a walk with me along the beach.

We didn't talk theology. I wasn't trying to argue, and I could tell they weren't either. But I needed to ask something I had carried quietly for years.

I turned to them and said, "Are you guys worried I'm going to hell? I don't want you to be afraid for me."

They paused, their eyes kind, their faces soft. Then they both said no. Not at all.

They didn't offer a theological disclaimer. They didn't try to walk it back or smooth it out.
They simply received the love in my question and met it with love of their own.

My dad said, "We trust God with you."

And my mom gently added, "What I trust about Jesus is so good... I just know I don't need to be afraid."

I didn't know if that meant their theology had shifted or if love won. But something in me relaxed, too. Something real and wise said, *Yes.* Because whatever God is—if it looks anything like Jesus, real or mythical—that had to be true. And that was good news.

We kept walking for a while, quietly, side by side, because sometimes silence *is* the conversation. My mom linked her arm through mine at one point. My dad gave my shoulder a little squeeze. Nothing dramatic. Just the kind of closeness that says, *We're still here. We still love you.*

That meant more than any words ever could, because I do love them. And I've never stopped wanting to be a good son—not in the performative, obedient sense, but in the deep sense that I care how my life affects theirs. I've never wanted to hurt them. Never wanted my freedom to feel like betrayal. I respect their faith. I respect how they live it. And I know their love for me flows through it.

That's the tension I live with: holding compassion for where they stand, while remaining honest about where I stand.

So to feel, in that moment, that they were okay—that they weren't afraid for me—that mattered more than I can say.

Because in the end, I don't think it's enough to seek freedom alone. Real liberation invites us into love—and real love holds space for the ones who matter most.

It hasn't always been easy.
We've had hard conversations. Some that got heated.
We've disagreed about politics, about justice, about the ways Michelle and I live and love. They've had to take in a lot of difficult, unfamiliar truths.
And we've made concessions too—choosing to keep some conversations open and some boundaries kind.

But through it all, we keep choosing each other.

It's not only my parents, either. Michelle's parents walked through all of it too. They were part of our church for fifteen of the sixteen years we led it. Imagine what it's like to be a parent watching that in real time—watching your daughter suffer, be misunderstood, wrestle, speak out, get brave, maybe make a few questionable decisions…or get some questionable tattoos.

That's not easy. And I'll always respect them for what it must have cost to carry that and stay in loving relationship with us through it all. Even when we walked away. Even when we burned it down. That's big, gracious, messy love.

Michelle's brothers—each in their own way—have been part of this journey too. We've had our moments, of course, but they've stayed connected. Showed up. Held space. Watched their sister evolve and stretch and change. They've still chosen relationship.

I know that's a lot. And I'm grateful.

And my sister—yeah, it's been hard there too. Back in 2013, we had a quasi-intense family debate over my changing beliefs about sexuality and gay marriage. Probably the gnarliest it's ever gotten in our family. Not a cage match, but tense. She and I don't live near each other, and we're *so* different. But we keep trying to love each other as best we can across that wide canyon. And I'm so thankful for that.

Whatever you want to call this—grace, maturity, divine mercy, or just a damn good family—I'm grateful.
Grateful for people who could have drawn a line and didn't.
Grateful for parents who were once my pastors and now are just my friends.

That's what I mean by still family.
Not perfect.
But still here.
Still holding on.
Still choosing love.

Over time, I've learned that you can stop believing what someone believes…and still believe in them. Still honor their sincerity. Still sit across the table without needing to win or convert.

I don't want to repeat the same old pattern by trading one form of exclusivism for another. I don't want to turn my exit into another entrance exam and start rejecting people because they are too conservative, too Christian, or too legalistic.

I'm trying to stay human.

I respect my friends who are people of faith. I want to live in a world where we can honor difference—real difference—without collapsing into the fluffy nonsense that "ultimately it's all the same."

It's not.
And facing that—without losing love—is the hard, grown-up work.

Just because the story didn't work for me anymore doesn't mean I have to rip someone else's hope out of their hands. That's not honesty. That's violence. Truth can be told without tearing, and love can hold space for difference without falling apart.

The bravest thing isn't converting each other or rejecting each other. It's holding our convictions while also loving and respecting those who see it differently.

We're still family.
All of us.
Even now.

CHAPTER 27
WHAT HOLDS ME NOW

"The great work now is to carry the presence of the divine
through the human journey, and not to ascend out of it."
—Miriam Macgillis

My life isn't built around institutional religious structures, supernatural beliefs, or ungrounded New-Age spirituality. But that doesn't mean I'm unheld.

Certain things still support me—practices, relationships, and ways of seeing—that help me approach life as sacred and meaningful. Not in a dogmatic way. Just in a lived, daily way. They remind me how to stay close to what's real. How to meet life as it is and respond with love.

I'm still held—by people, practices, and ways of seeing that keep me close to what's real. By relationships where we don't need to fix each other, by truth-telling friendships, brave conversations, and quiet repair. The sacred didn't disappear when the theology collapsed. It just showed up differently.

Here's what I've found still holds me, even in the space beyond religion.

Other religious traditions hold me.
While I don't necessarily subscribe to their metaphysics, I recognize the wisdom embedded in their practices. More than belief systems, they're

technologies of the soul—rituals, stories, postures, and disciplines that help humans live with more awareness, inspiration, humility, and care.

I no longer feel the need to choose one or defend it. I let them speak to me where they're wise. I borrow language when it fits and leave the rest.

Sometimes that wisdom comes through Taoist stillness, sometimes through Buddhist compassion, sometimes through Indigenous reverence for the land, and sometimes through the contemplative silence at the heart of Christian mysticism.

One example among many is the Tao. It reminds me that forcing outcomes rarely leads to real transformation. That water is more powerful than stone—not by strength, but by flow. That surrender isn't defeat. It's alignment.

I don't feel pressure to believe in Lao Tzu's legendary virgin birth. But I do feel the quiet pull of the Tao's invitation to live in harmony with *what is.*

Somewhere in me, the old Judeo-Christian language of salvation and redemption still speaks—not as doctrine, but as a reminder that renewal is possible. In a world of noise and pressure and proving, both voices call me back to the same kind of trust—to act without striving, to let meaning arise without needing to control it, to remember that renewal and return are, in the end, the same motion.

Psychedelics hold me.
Not because they gave me all the answers—but because they helped me start asking better questions. They've opened me to awe and wonder and beauty beyond words. But more importantly, they've exposed the ways I get in my own way.

I've met the sacred in those spaces. But I've also met the parts of me that grasp, that hide, that pretend. They've brought me face to face with my control patterns, my fears of not being enough, my habit of staying in my head instead of in my life.

Again and again, I've felt the ego relax its grip—not vanish, just soften. I don't buy the whole ego-death mythology. The only people I've met whose egos truly died are wrapped in bodies that did too.

What actually happens, if I'm paying attention, is that the volume of self-protection gets turned down just enough for love to get a word in. For gratitude to express itself. And for a kind of wholeness I can't manufacture with effort.

After the peak fades, the real work begins.
Integration. Shadow work. Pattern breaking.
Learning how to live from what I saw.
Learning how to bring the light I saw into hard conversations, into parenting, into my marriage, into my work.

It's become part of the work I do now, helping others live what they saw too.

That's what holds me now: not just the vision, but the practice.

Embodied sexuality holds me.
At times, I've approached sex as a way to relax.
To feel close. To get comfort.
And sometimes, that's still true.
But now I know it can be so much more than that.

Sex, for me, has become a kind of practice. A place where presence meets intensity. Where honesty gets tested. Where the body stops lying. It's not a performance or an escape, but rather a portal into something elemental.

Into vitality. Eros. Aliveness.

Beyond simply desire, it's about energy. The same current that animates creativity, connection, and spiritual clarity moves through erotic experience too—if I'm awake enough to notice.

Sexuality is life force. And every time I repress it, numb it, or hide from it, some part of me starts to wither. To shrink back from the world. To participate in my own slow death.

But when I engage it honestly—not just as an act, but as a transmission of truth—it brings me back to life. It roots me in my body. It shows me where I'm still armored. It teaches me how to give and receive without control. To be exposed, and to be okay with that. To stay present on the edge.

Sometimes it's awkward or intense, even funny in its vulnerability. And sometimes it takes me to the edge of myself, closer to truth than comfort. It's one of the most intimate mirrors I know. The way I show up here—attuned or distracted, generous or guarded—usually reflects how I'm showing up everywhere else.

Underneath the pleasure and the vulnerability, there's raw creative potential.
To *become* something.
To move energy.
To meet life more fully.
To stop holding back.

❧

I don't see it as separate from my spiritual path anymore. In its most honest form, it takes me to the edge of myself—and sometimes beyond. Instead of an escape from reality, it allows me to touch something more real than I usually let in.

The deeper I go, the more I realize that making love, at its best, isn't about technique or tension or even climax—it's about soul recognition. The meeting of two beings who, for a moment, drop all pretense and remember that they belong to something vast, tender, and alive; to something infinite, beautiful, and temporary.

So I treat it like a practice.
A practice for presence. For embodiment. For becoming.

Science holds me.
Science is a living process rather than a closed system of facts. It's a way of staying curious and accountable to what *is*.

The key has been learning how to hold knowledge without losing humility, wonder, and awe. Science, at its best, keeps us honest. But science without wonder can become as myopic as religion without love. Too often, scientific materialism treats life as a meaningless heap of data to decode rather than an unfolding mystery that calls for our full presence in every encounter. In that sense, fundamentalist religion and hard materialism share a blind spot: both cling to certainty. One sanctifies it, the other sterilizes it. Either way, the mystery gets lost.

I don't need to eliminate mystery to be inspired by scientific discoveries. I don't have to disenchant the cosmos in order to maintain rational inquiry. But I also don't need a supernatural explanation to feel reverence.

The sacred is here. In the dirt and the details. In quarks and nebulas. In bacteria and protozoa. In the 4.5-billion-year experiment where earth has transformed molten rock into Shakespeare, giraffes, and redwood forests. The sacred is in my body. In nature. In the trust of another person. In the birth of my children.

I just have to pay attention.

The more I learn about the universe, the more reverent I become. The more I study biology, consciousness, and emergence, the more I glimpse the numinous beneath the measurable.

And it holds me to remember: I am evolution. A temporary expression of an ongoing story. From atoms to ecosystems, reality is made of relationships. Connection is the medium of existence.

So if nothing else, the inherent purpose of my life is to participate in the unfolding of relationship itself. To tend, to listen, to adapt, to stay open. Surrendering to what life is doing—rather than resisting it—has become a sacred practice.

Many of the things that once held my faith still hold me now—just differently.

Music still moves me, but it's no longer a tool for worshipping a supernatural Being. It's medicine. Memory. A way to feel without filtering. Certain songs hit like scripture, except now, they don't tell me what to believe. They remind me I'm human and sweep me away in vibrational magic carpet rides of ecstasy.

Community still matters deeply, but not the kind built on shared beliefs and conformity. Now I look for people who can tell the truth, sit in the unknown, and laugh easily. I've stopped needing everyone to agree with me. I want to feel safe enough to be real and brave enough to offer the same.

Structure still supports me, but it's self-chosen now. No more cramming my life into a spiritual performance calendar. Now it's beach walks, daily gym time, stillness, time in nature, journaling, good sleep. It's structure that makes space for what matters.

Language still holds me, but I use it more like clay than stone. I don't need to lock ideas down. I want to stay in conversation with them. Words have become invitations instead of answers.

My parents still hold me, not through theology, but through ongoing relationship. They've shown me how love can outlast belief and how grace shows up face to face.

And longing—the deep ache I used to think could only be satisfied by God—that still pulses in me. But now, I see it as a gift. Not a hunger for heaven, but a compass for what's real, beautiful, and worth showing up for.

Looking back, I used to organize my life (and our church) around five core purposes straight out of *The Purpose Driven Life (& Church)* by Rick Warren: worship, fellowship, discipleship, ministry, and evangelism. These purposes gave clarity and direction to life and to our community.

And what's cool? They still hold up. The language shifts slightly, and I certainly don't need a Bible verse to back them up, but these central pillars of a life of meaning can still shape how I measure and live out my values.

So I've reframed them below. Not as duties to fulfill, but as practices for life that keep me honest, connected, and open.

1. Worship becomes *awe*.

Not toward a distant deity, but toward this moment. This glorious sunrise. The mystery I get to live inside.

2. Fellowship becomes *community*.

Community built on shared humanity, not shared doctrine. A place where we can be seen, known, and real.

3. Discipleship becomes *character*.

Not becoming someone else's version of good, but becoming more fully myself—aligned with my values of integrity, humility, and love.

4. Ministry becomes *service*.

Service based on alignment, not obligation, threat of punishment, or promise of eternal reward. Where my joy meets someone else's need, I try to show up.

5. Evangelism becomes *embodiment*.

I'm no longer interested in converting others, but in becoming someone worth trusting. Letting my life speak, without needing to argue. A living inspiration. I want to invite a fascination built on the actual pragmatic value of a beautiful life.

These are the various things that hold me now. Some are simply ordinary and earthy, some are philosophical, some are deeply experiential.

And you know what? I'll bet they keep changing. At this point, these are the tools I've chosen and practices I return to.

As I compare what holds me now with what held me decades ago, I can appreciate how all the beauty my old worldview offered me is available on the other side—but without the fear, the threat, the control, or the implausibility.

The essence is there, but the trappings are gone. The limited, temporary, and at times toxic framework of religion has dropped away, like a cocoon after metamorphosis.

Stephen Jenkinson once said, "Human beings are made, not born." While we're biologically complete at birth, psychospiritually, we are wildly unfinished. There's no autopilot into maturity. Becoming human is inconvenient, costly, and sacred.

We live in a culture that offers almost no support for that process. So instead of becoming, we perform. We curate. We chase highs. We numb. Even religion—ironically—can become a beautiful distraction from actually facing ourselves.

But real spirituality shouldn't pull us out of life. It should take us deeper into it. It should break the spell of escape and invite us to stay.

I suppose that this is what I mean when I say something holds me. It's not a god or a theology. It's not a sense of certainty or superiority. It's the ordinary, evolutionary, ongoing work of becoming more fully human.

CHAPTER 28
A DEEPER THANKS

"The primary prayer is one of awe, and it is probably the most effective prayer because through it we turn to our origins and just behold with a sense of gratitude."

—Brian Swimme

Gratitude, for me, came in the quiet. In the aftermath. In the stretch of time where everything had fallen away, and I was still here.

I used to think gratitude was something you had to feel. Now I think it's something you can choose. It's just… available.

There are mornings when nothing's resolved. The questions still swirl. The body still aches. The world still feels heavy.

But the light spills through the window anyway.
My son laughs in the other room.
Michelle hands me coffee with that half-smile that says we've made it through worse.
And something softens in me.
Not everything. But enough.

I don't feel grateful for everything. That's never been the goal. I feel grateful *in* it. Grateful in the mess. In the questions. In the ordinary morning light. Grateful for what I can touch. For what I can give. For what is still mine to love.

This moment.
This heartbeat.
This body.
This chance to be here and say yes again.

Gratitude is a way of relating to the world without needing it to change.
It shows up not in the high moments, but in the small ones.
In the quiet reach across the sheets.
In the last few bites of dinner.
In the sound of the ocean reminding me I'm not in charge of anything that matters.

I don't say thank you because everything is perfect.
I say it because I'm here.
And sometimes, that's enough.

There's a kind of gratitude that doesn't need a source. The philosopher John Caputo writes that a true gift has no giver. If it has a giver, he says, then it comes with strings. Expectations. An invisible ledger.

But a true gift just arrives. No return address. No terms and conditions.

Life, I'm starting to believe, is that kind of gift. Instead of being a prize for good behavior or a reward for belief, it's just... here. Given without explanation. Offered without demand.

There's a kind of freedom in that. It means I don't have to prove I deserve it. I don't have to understand it to receive it. I can say thank you without needing to direct my words anywhere.

Sometimes I whisper it to the clouds.
Sometimes to my body.
Sometimes into the silence.

And whether or not anyone's listening, it still matters that I said it. Because that's what gratitude has become for me. A rhythm of reverence rather than an affirmation of certainty. A way of saying: *I'm here and I'm paying attention.*

I remember a walk I took one morning in Bend. The forest was still damp from early rain, and the air had that mix of pine and earth that always makes me feel like I'm being let in on a secret. No podcast. No playlist. Just footsteps on soft ground and the wind threading through branches.

I stopped. I was surrounded by trees that didn't need anything from me. They weren't impressed by my past. They weren't asking for belief. They were just *being*—alive, grounded, patient.

And I felt it. That subtle, cellular kind of gratitude. Simply for the privilege of being part of this.

This world that doesn't wait for our theology to bloom. This moss-covered silence. This breath, this morning, in this body—still tethered to the pulse of something ancient and wordless and good.

I didn't say anything out loud, but I felt the words move through me like breath.

Thank you.

Not as obligation. Not as transaction. As truth.

That moment gave me a reference point, a feeling I've returned to over and over: Gratitude doesn't need to be shouted. Sometimes it just needs to be noticed.

A few Christmases ago, we had all the kids home. That doesn't happen much anymore. The older two are out living their lives—busy and beautiful in ways I'm proud of and still aching to hold close. But that day, for a few hours, they were all here.

At some point, in the chaos of wrapping paper and leftovers, we all ended up on the floor. Sprawled across the carpet. Tangled in blankets and limbs and conversation.

I pulled them close, one by one, and closed my eyes. And there it was again. That silent, overwhelming wave of thank you.

For the miracle.
For the sweetness.
For the fleeting, stupid beauty of it all.

Gratitude not in spite of the fact that it would end but rather because it will.

That's the strange magic of paying attention: The more you realize it won't last, the more you actually show up for it.

I didn't need the moment to stay.
I just needed to be in it. Fully.
And I was.

That, too, is gratitude.
I'm not in control.
I'm not permanent.
But I was here when it mattered.

That's a gift.

Sometimes I think the reason gratitude is so hard for us is because we're terrified of loss. And maybe rightly so.

To be grateful is to admit it's all temporary.
To feel the sweetness while knowing it will pass.
To love a life you don't get to keep.

But isn't that what makes it beautiful?

We spend so much of our time afraid of life, worried about what we could lose.
Guess what? You do lose in the end. Everything. It's a given.
In the end, you die. And everything you've collected is ash.
Let that liberate your desire and free you of fear.

Thanks to Death, you have nothing to lose.
Live your life playfully. It's all house money.
Let your mortality be what makes you invincible.

Do you even really see a flower unless you see that it will wither? Do you even really feel the presence of your child unless you know—somewhere deep down—that they won't always be curled against your chest, that these snuggles are numbered?

Sometimes when I tuck the boys in at night, I remember that. I kiss them, smell their hair, press my eyelashes against their cheeks. And I let the truth in:
None of us live forever.
Someday I will die.
Someday they will, too.

Not to be morbid.
But to be in my right mind.

Because when you stop pretending life will last forever, you start to see what's actually here. You stop taking it all for granted. The warmth. The mess. The breath. The miracle that any of it ever happened.

And when we allow room to not know the answers—to really not know—something opens. We live in the tension of uncertainty. Maybe there's something after this. Maybe there isn't. But either way, we stop putting our living on layaway for some "second level" that may never come. It brings us intensely into the present moment, into the absolute miracle that being conscious in this world is.

It's not nothing... and it might be everything.

Grief is often the moment we realize we've been on the take.
That we treated the gift like it was owed.
That we forgot to say thank you.

But gratitude—real, embodied gratitude—is how we come back to our senses. It's how we live before the eulogy. It's how we bow to what's passing, even as we hold it.

So take a deep breath.
Remind yourself that one day, it will be your last.

And then go out and live like it's all a gift.
Because it is.
Even now.
Especially now.

Lately, I've started doing this quiet little thing in my head.

As I move through the day—maybe chatting with Dodge about space or watching Ace melt into a bowl of ice cream—I imagine I've lost my memory. I picture my future self—older and softer—being reintroduced to the people I love.

It's me, but senile.

"This is your son Dodge. He loves space and plays guitar. He's witty and sharp, and a loyal friend."

"This is your son Ace. Gentle. Deeply tuned into the emotions of others. Recently he's become a huge Sublime fan."

"This is Jaeger. He makes us laugh in ways no one else can. He's in his twenties now, but he still gives hugs like a kid who never learned how to let go."

"This is Riley. She's fire and heart, go-getter and underdog-defender, stunning inside and out. Life of the party. More tender than she lets on. Always doing her best."

And then:
"This is Michelle. Your wife. Your best friend. You've loved her since she was sixteen. You grew up together. Died and rose again together. Raised four incredible souls. Her love is the closest thing to God you've ever known. Be so good to her. Cherish her."

Maybe it sounds simple. But it resets me. It reawakens the wonder.

Because love, when it's familiar, can start to blur. But seen through the eyes of someone meeting them again for the first time, it's overwhelming. It's pure gift.

And that, more than anything, is why I say thank you.
Because life is happening, and I get to be here for it.

Hand over heart.
One more time.

Thank you.
I love you.

CHAPTER 29
FOUND MY SOUL

"The soul is a person's unique place in the world—
their ecological niche—and the calling to live it out."
—Bill Plotkin

"Soul is revealed in attachment, love, and community; in music,
food, clothing, home, and landscape. It is not a separate thing
but the style with which we live life."
—Thomas Moore

My soul wasn't missing. It was buried.
Under performance.
Under doctrine.
Under the need to be useful, right, and admired.

And cancer, and loss, and love—they dug me out.
Not all at once. Not cleanly.
But just enough to hear what was buried beneath belief:
Still here.

I lost my faith.
I killed my church.
I saved my life.

And somewhere in the rubble—between the grief, the silence, and the
strange beauty of being unneeded—I found something I didn't even
know I'd lost: A deeper self. A gentle knowing.

I found my soul.

I used to think of the soul as a theological idea—something you either saved or lost, depending on what you believed.

Now I think of it more like poetry. Not a ghost living in my body or a prize to win in the afterlife, but the name we give to the part of us that won't settle for half a life.

Bill Plotkin calls the soul your "ecological niche"—the unique way you belong to the world. It's not something hidden inside, but rather it's revealed when your outer life aligns with your inner truth. It's a participation, a way of being at home in the unfolding story of Earth.

We often speak of places or things as having soul or maybe being soulless. In that sense, soul is the depth and vitality in a thing or a person. Not something that floats above it, but something that sinks below.

Along with poetry, I also think of the soul as a weight. The soul isn't flashy. It doesn't win arguments. It's what gives a moment gravity and what you feel in someone who's been undone and lived to tell the truth. It's the earned density that comes from being cracked open by life and staying open.

There's a kind of false depth that passes for wisdom—the guru performance, the curated mystic, the charismatic preacher.
But the soul doesn't preach; it listens.
And it doesn't lift you above others; it roots you among them.

Without soul, we feel empty; we have shallow lives devoid of meaning and power, detached from the world and others.

I've touched whatever soul is in psychedelic space and sexual ecstasy—those rare moments when the ego dissolves and something ancient, tender, and vast moves through you. Where nothing is separate, and love isn't an idea—it's a force.

That's not theoretical. That's not doctrinal. That's contact.

Is there such a thing as an *eternal* soul? I don't know. Maybe. It's not something I can prove or disprove. But if anything endures, I hope it's made of love.

Maybe the better question is this:
Are we living lives beautiful enough to be eternal?

The soul I discovered after the systems collapsed, after the titles and doctrines were gone, after my gods were dead, wasn't a destination. It was a direction.

It tugged at me.
A knowing that lived in my bones.
Something that didn't need belief to be real.

I didn't find that in church or in theology. I found it in the woods. In some calm place inside me that could sense the sacred in little things. In Michelle's hands. In grief. In cause-less joy. In the moments that didn't ask for performance—only my attention.

It was a return to the life that fits.
To the way of being that makes me feel most alive.
To the thread that's been pulling at me all along.

Call it soul or don't. Whatever it is, it's mine to follow. I may never name it perfectly, but I know when I'm walking with it because it's always whispering, *This matters.*

I think soul might be what I am when I'm most alive.
And to that—whatever it is—
I'm listening.

CHAPTER 30
LIFE IS A GIFT.
LOVE IS THE POINT.

"To live is enough"
—Shunryu Suzuki

I didn't set out to lose my faith. Or my church. Or my certainty. But I did.

And in the rubble, I found something more reliable:
The wild, terrifying beauty of not knowing—and living anyway.

I found the courage to turn off the supernatural night light. To spit out the pacifier of certainty and look at life, as it is, and call it good. To appreciate the gift of being alive and to respond in gratitude and love.

Sacred anyway.

Over time the uncertainty that used to feel scary, unmoored, and isolating became a comfort. I could just accept it and wrap it around me like a fleece blanket. I could actually feel a particular kind of faith emerge. A way of trusting in reality beyond control.

I had lost my religion, but not my longing.

And from there I could just ask what kind of person I wanted to be in the face of that. That's where that mantra that came to me through cancer became a guiding light.

Life is a gift.
Love is the point.

Again, when I say life is a gift, I don't mean there's a giver in the sky handing it out. I mean that life, in all its fragility and mystery, can be received with the kind of reverence we usually reserve for sacred things. A sunrise doesn't need a sender to be beautiful. A breath doesn't need a backstory to be holy.

Calling life a gift is about posturing the heart toward gratitude, even in the absence of certainty.

And yes, I know it might sound strange to say thank you to a sunset, or whisper love to the wind—but something in us is wired to relate. We're built for connection. When we speak to the world—not as object, but as presence—we remember that we belong. This isn't just scenery. It's kin. Gratitude becomes a way of coming home to the wider body of life.

And then, love is the point.

That's the phrase that kept echoing through me in the aftermath of it all—in the silence of post-church life, in the quiet of Encinitas mornings, in the laughter of my kids around a kitchen table no longer burdened by Sunday prep.

These aren't just poetic ideas. They're deeply practical.
"Life is a gift" invites gratitude.
"Love is the point" calls us to compassion.

They're postures. Ways of leaning in. When we live with them at the center, we're more rooted. More human. More whole.

From these postures come the imperatives:
Give thanks.
Give love.

And from those, the mantras:
Thank you.
I love you.

Each one flows into the next—postures, imperatives, mantras—forming a living circle. Gratitude nourishes love. Love expresses itself through thanks. The circle deepens.

This framework is deceptively simple, which is what makes it so potent. It doesn't require theology. It doesn't demand cosmic certainty or metaphysical gymnastics. It doesn't manipulate through guilt or bypass through positivity slogans.

This is a spirituality of presence.
It honors mystery without needing to solve it.
It encourages growth without trapping us in a fixed identity.
It invites meaning without insisting on control.

Meaning isn't something to discover out there. It's available right here—in attention, in kindness, in aliveness.

There's no need to seek the meaning *of* life when there is so much meaning *in* life. Nature and love are enough. We can tell life what it means to us, then live like that matters.

This realization came through loss—through stripping it all down to what still held weight. And what remained, after certainty and spiritual scaffolding collapsed, was love.

Not the sentimental kind. Not the slogan.
Fierce, soul-honest love.

The kind that doesn't need to win arguments or claim divine authority.
The kind that listens more than it speaks.
That stays with the moment.
That walks people home without insisting they take your path.

Love, I've come to believe, is the only spiritual authority that matters. Why? Because it's real. It humbles our theology. It disrupts our self-righteousness. It grounds us in the now.

It's what helped me stay when I wanted to run.
What helped me let go when I was clinging.
What carried Michelle and me through impossible conversations and into new expressions of intimacy and family we hadn't seen modeled but somehow knew were true.

Love is a practice.
And for me, it's become the measure of what's worth keeping.

Do I feel more alive?
Am I more honest?
Is this helping me love with more freedom and integrity?

If yes—keep going.
If no—release it.
That's the compass now.

This doesn't mean I have it all figured out. I still get scared. Still slip into performance. Still struggle to trust my own voice.

But love is patient.
It invites us to begin again. And again. And again.

And when everything else fades—when the titles are gone, the sermons quiet, the crowds disappear—what remains is whether we loved well. Whether we told the truth. Whether we showed up with open hearts.

Love isn't just the point. It's the only thing worth dying for.

And I don't mean some grand gesture. I mean dying with the quiet confidence that I didn't betray myself to keep the peace. That I didn't perform my way through life. That I didn't trade my soul for applause or safety.

I want to die never having abandoned myself for belonging.
I want to die awake.
With my hand in Michelle's.
With my kids knowing they're seen and pursued and delighted in.
That I'm here to love and support whoever they want to be and however they build a life.

Love is the point. And death reminds us not to wait.

That's the strange gift of mortality—it collapses the illusion that we have endless time to postpone being fully ourselves. It clears the clutter. It makes the urgent things obvious.

When I was sick during chemo, and even more so after, I saw how much time I'd spent trying to belong in places I'd already outgrown. And how little of that effort really mattered.

In an interview not long after, I said something that still feels true: Death became my teacher because I wanted to live in such a way that I could die without regret. Cancer beautifully revealed this paradox.

When you get diagnosed with something life threatening, it's natural to feel robbed. *Hey—this isn't how I wanted to go.*

But that realization—*I don't want to die like this*—immediately invites a question: *Then how do I want to die?*

And sitting with that question long enough has a strange effect. Because the way you want to die tells you exactly how you're meant to live.

I realized I didn't want to die fighting for more time or trying to prove anything. I wanted to die saying *I love you* to everyone who mattered. I wanted my last words to match the deepest truth of my life. And once I knew that, it became clear: The only way to die that way is to live that way now.

To wastefully give all the love I had without reservation.
To know I had told the truth.
That I had chosen presence.
That I emptied myself in a living ritual of gratitude and love.

So I ask myself often:
Am I showing up fully, without withholding anything?
Am I living from my truth, not my mask?
Am I in gratitude rather than scarcity?
Am I speaking from my heart instead of my fear?

If the answer is yes—even in part—I keep going.

These are not beliefs.
They're a way of saying yes to life.

The virtues:
Gratitude. Love.

The imperatives:
Give thanks. Give love.

The mantras:
Thank you. I love you.

Put your hand over your heart and feel.
Say it to yourself.
To a friend.
To the sunset.
To the meal.
To your body.
To this moment.
To life itself.

Because that's all we need now.
Not certainty. Not safety.
Just alignment—with what's real, and love.

There's no destination. We are already here.
It's this moment. Right here.
No formula. Just the next loving thing.

I don't need to understand the mystery to stand in awe of it.

Life is a gift. Love is the point.

SONGS THAT CARRIED US

Throughout our journey, certain songs resonated deeply with Michelle and me. I've mentioned a few in this book, but there were many more—honest, raw, pain-informed, freedom-focused anthems that gave words to what we were living. We've gathered them into a playlist called *Life Is a Gift. Love Is the Point* on Spotify. We hope they speak to you as they did to us.

ENDNOTES

Introductory Page

- Dante Alighieri, *The Divine Comedy: Inferno*, Canto I, lines 1–3. Translated by Allen Mandelbaum, Bantam Books, 1982.

- Anne Lamott, "Anne Lamott: Falling Off the Tightrope," Beliefnet, June 2006, https://www.beliefnet.com/faiths/christianity/2006/06/anne-lamott-falling-off-the-tightrope.aspx

Chapter 1

- James P. Carse, The Religious Case Against Belief (New York: Penguin Books, 2008), 61.

- David Bazan, "Little Landslide," *Blanco* (Barsuk Records, 2016).

Chapter 2

- Frederick Buechner, *Telling the Truth: The Gospel as Tragedy, Comedy, and Fairy Tale* (Harper & Row, 1977).

Chapter 3

- Mary Oliver, "Wild Geese," in *Dream Work* (Atlantic Monthly Press, 1986).

Chapter 4

- Ken Wilber, *A Brief History of Everything* (Boston: Shambhala Publications, 1996), 69. Quote is a paraphrase I heard him say at his house in 2014, speaking to a group of ministers.

- Loyal D. Rue, from *Religion Is Not About God: How Spiritual Traditions Nurture Our Biological Nature and What to Expect When They Fail* (New Brunswick, NJ: Rutgers University Press, 2005), 2–3, 256–57.

Chapter 5

- Friedrich Nietzsche, *Beyond Good and Evil: Prelude to a Philosophy of the Future*, trans. Walter Kaufmann (New York: Vintage Books, 1989), 69.
- The quote by Jesus is paraphrased from John 20:29.

Chapter 6

- Alfred Tennyson, *In Memoriam A.H.H.* (London: Edward Moxon, 1850), Canto 96, line 11.

Chapter 7

- The introductory quote is widely attributed to Chögyam Trungpa Rinpoche, although the original source is unknown.
- Bible quotations from 1 Samuel 15:2–3 and Exodus 32:27, New International Version®, NIV® Copyright ©1973, 1978, 1984, 2011 by Biblica, Inc.® Used by permission. All rights reserved worldwide.
- Ken Wilber, *One Taste: The Journals of Ken Wilber, 1999–2000* (Boston: Shambhala Publications, 2000), 27.

Chapter 8

- U2, "Every Breaking Wave," *Songs of Innocence* (Island Records, 2014).

Chapter 9

- The introductory quote is generally attributed to Stacie Martin. See, for example, "Tiny Buddha: Simple Wisdom for Complex Lives," https://tinybuddha.com/quotes/tiny-buddha-you-can-stand-up-for-anything-that-you-believe-in-but-if-you-cant-find-the-courage-to-stand-alone-it-wont-really-matter-what-you-believe/.
- Elizabeth Dias, "Inside the Evangelical Fight Over Gay Marriage," *TIME Magazine*, January 26, 2015, p. 39.

Chapter 10

- Nina Riggs, *The Bright Hour: A Memoir of Living and Dying* (New York: Simon & Schuster, 2017), 6.

- F. Scott Fitzgerald, *The Great Gatsby* (New York: Charles Scribner's Sons, 1925), 161.

- Aaron Sternke, "Madness," performed by Fell From a Star, on *Madness – Single* (Seattle, WA: independent release, 2014), digital audio recording.

Chapter 11

- Rebecca Campbell, *Light Is the New Black: A Guide to Answering Your Soul's Calling and Working Your Light* (Carlsbad, CA: Hay House, 2015), 79.

- Nick Hornby, *A Long Way Down* (New York: Riverhead Books, 2005), 85.

Chapter 12

- Peter Rollins, *The Fidelity of Betrayal: Towards a Church Beyond Belief* (Brewster, MA: Paraclete Press, 2008), 1.

Chapter 13

- Dietrich Bonhoeffer, *Letters and Papers from Prison*, edited by Eberhard Bethge (New York: Macmillan, 1972), 360. (From Bonhoeffer's letter to Eberhard Bethge, July 16, 1944.).

- Meister Eckhart, Sermon 52, in *Meister Eckhart: The Essential Sermons, Commentaries, Treatises, and Defense*, translated and edited by Edmund Colledge and Bernard McGinn (New York: Paulist Press, 1981), 200.

Chapter 14

- C. S. Lewis, letter to Arthur Greeves, October 18, 1931, in The Collected Letters of C. S. Lewis, Vol. 1 (San Francisco: HarperSanFrancisco, 2004), 977.

- Kent Dobson, *The Christ Symbol* (Grand Rapids, MI: Arimos Press, 2021), 8, 35.
- C. S. Lewis, letter to Arthur Greeves, October 18, 1931, in *The Collected Letters of C. S. Lewis, Vol. 1* (San Francisco: HarperSanFrancisco, 2004), 977.
- Dorothy Day, quoted in Robert Ellsberg, *Dorothy Day: Selected Writings* (Maryknoll, NY: Orbis Books, 1992), 175.
- Thich Nhat Hanh, *Peace Is Every Step: The Path of Mindfulness in Everyday Life* (New York: Bantam Books, 1991), 81.
- A. A. Milne, *Winnie-the-Pooh* (London: Methuen & Co., 1926), chap. 4.
- Paramahansa Yogananda, *Man's Eternal Quest: Collected Talks and Essays, Vol. 1* (Los Angeles: Self-Realization Fellowship, 1954), 3.
- Pema Chödrön, *The Places That Scare You: A Guide to Fearlessness in Difficult Times* (Boston: Shambhala Publications, 2001), 91.
- J. R. R. Tolkien, *The Fellowship of the Ring* (Boston: Houghton Mifflin, 1954), Book I, chap. 2, "The Shadow of the Past."
- Martin Luther King Jr., *Strength to Love* (New York: Harper & Row, 1963), 53.
- Jesus of Nazareth, paraphrased from Matthew 5:3–10 and Luke 6:27.

Chapter 15

- Paramahansa Yogananda, *The Second Coming of Christ: The Resurrection of the Christ Within You, Vol. 1* (Los Angeles: Self-Realization Fellowship, 2004), 11.
- John Shelby Spong, *Why Christianity Must Change or Die: A Bishop Speaks to Believers in Exile* (San Francisco: HarperSanFrancisco, 1998), 129.
- The quote about absurdities and atrocities is generally attributed to Voltaire, although the original wording is uncertain; see https://www.cato.org/publications/commentary/origins-warning-from-voltaire for further discussion.

Chapter 16

- Sam Harris, *Waking Up: A Guide to Spirituality Without Religion* (New York: Simon & Schuster, 2014), 25.
- Kester Brewin, *After Magic: Moves Beyond SuperNature, From Batman to Shakespeare* (London: VAUX Books, 2013).
- Robert G. Ingersoll, *The Liberty of Man, Woman and Child* (New York: C. P. Farrell, 1877), 27.

Chapter 17

- Johann Wolfgang von Goethe, "The Holy Longing," in *Goethe's Poems*, translated by John Frederick Nims (Princeton, NJ: Princeton University Press, 1998), 131.
- Bruce Sanguin, *The Way of the Wind: The Path and Practice of Evolutionary Christian Mysticism* (Vancouver, BC: Castle Quay Books, 2012), 223.
- Brian Swimme, *The Universe Is a Green Dragon: A Cosmic Creation Story* (Santa Fe, NM: Bear & Company, 1984), 43; and Brian Swimme and Mary Evelyn Tucker, *Journey of the Universe* (New Haven, CT: Yale University Press, 2011), 136.

Chapter 18

- David Whyte, "Self-Portrait," in *Fire in the Earth* (Langley, WA: Many Rivers Press, 1992), 23–24.
- Thomas Merton, *Conjectures of a Guilty Bystander* (New York: Doubleday, 1966), 208.
- *The Goonies*, directed by Richard Donner (Los Angeles: Warner Bros., 1985)

Chapter 19

- Thich Nhat Hanh, *Peace Is Every Step: The Path of Mindfulness in Everyday Life* (New York: Bantam Books, 1991), 12.

Chapter 20

- Martin Buber, *I and Thou*, translated by Walter Kaufmann (New York: Charles Scribner's Sons, 1970), 62.

- Bruce Sanguin, *Dismantled: How Love and Psychedelics Broke a Clergyman Apart and Put Him Back Together* (Vancouver, BC: Green Spirit Press, 2021), 241.

Chapter 21

- Ozzy Osbourne, "Life Won't Wait," track 8 on *Scream* (Epic Records, 2010). Lyrics by Ozzy Osbourne, Kevin Churko, and Adam Wakeman.

Chapter 22

- Mary Oliver, "The Journey," in *Dream Work* (Boston: Atlantic Monthly Press, 1986), 38.

Chapter 23

- Joan Didion, *Slouching Towards Bethlehem* (New York: Farrar, Straus and Giroux, 1968), 138.

Chapter 24

- Stanislav Grof, *The Holotropic Mind: The Three Levels of Human Consciousness and How They Shape Our Lives*, with Hal Zina Bennett (New York: HarperCollins, 1993), 6.

- *The Village*, directed by M. Night Shyamalan (United States: Touchstone Pictures/Blinding Edge Pictures, 2004).

- T. S. Eliot, *Collected Poems*, 1909–1962 (London: Faber and Faber, 1963), 77. Originally from "Little Gidding," Four Quartets (1942).

Chapter 25

- Jorge Luis Borges, "Praise," in *Selected Poems, 1923–1967*, edited by Norman Thomas di Giovanni (New York: Delta, 1973), 133.

- Sabrina Claudio, "Before It's Too Late," on *No Rain, No Flowers* (SC Entertainment, 2018).

Chapter 26

- James P. Carse, *The Silence of God: Meditations on Prayer* (New York: Simon & Schuster, 1985), 34.

Chapter 27

- Miriam MacGillis, quoted in Thomas Berry and Brian Swimme, *The Universe Story: From the Primordial Flaring Forth to the Ecozoic Era—A Celebration of the Unfolding of the Cosmos* (San Francisco: HarperSanFrancisco, 1992), 258.

- Rick Warren, *The Purpose Driven Life: What on Earth Am I Here For?* (Grand Rapids, MI: Zondervan, 2012).

- Rick Warren, *The Purpose Driven Church: Growth without Compromising Your Message and Mission* (Grand Rapids, MI: Zondervan, 2007).

- Stephen Jenkinson, *Die Wise: A Manifesto for Sanity and Soul* (Berkeley, CA: North Atlantic Books, 2015), 79.

Chapter 28

- Brian Swimme, *The Hidden Heart of the Cosmos: Humanity and the New Story* (Maryknoll, NY: Orbis Books, 1996), 92.

Chapter 29

- Bill Plotkin, *Nature and the Human Soul: Cultivating Wholeness and Community in a Fragmented World* (Novato, CA: New World Library, 2008), 43.

- Thomas Moore, *Care of the Soul: A Guide for Cultivating Depth and Sacredness in Everyday Life* (New York: HarperCollins, 1992), 5.

Chapter 30

- Shunryu Suzuki, *Zen Mind, Beginner's Mind* (New York: Weatherhill, 1970), 92.

ACKNOWLEDGMENTS

This book would not exist without the slow undoing and wild remaking of my life. Thank you to everyone who stood with me—when I was dying, and when I began again. Your presence, your patience, your fierce love helped shape the words on these pages far more than any writing session ever did. This isn't just my story—it's a shared one.

To Michelle: My partner, my witness, my co-conspirator in both collapse and becoming. We've been walking this road together since we were teenagers, learning how to grow up while still holding hands. There is no version of this story without you. You've loved me through fire and silence, through doubt and joy, through every version of me I've had to outgrow. And just as much, you've trusted me with your own becoming: with the shedding of layers, the opening of old armor, the slow revealing of the woman you already were beneath it all. Thank you for letting me see you. For choosing connection over protection. For walking beside me and reminding me how to love what's real. I'm still in awe of you.

To our big kids, the OG's, Riley and Jaeger: Thank you for growing up inside the whirlwind. You've lived through our transformation as much as we have. You watched your parents become different people—sometimes slowly, sometimes all at once—and you held it together with us through cancer, through uncertainty, through the deep undoing of so much we once thought was solid. I know it wasn't always easy. And still, you loved us. You adapted. You kept showing up. You have more strength and grace in you than I had at your age, and I'm in awe of the humans you're becoming.

To our "littles," Dodge and Ace: Thank you for completing our family halfway through the story. Your innocence and joy lifted us all when things were heavy. You brought levity, play, and wonder into the hardest chapters. You've grown into young men of strength and tenderness who know how to love and feel. I can't think of anything the world needs more than that.

To all four kids: We're so proud of who you are and who you're becoming. And we hope—deep in your bones—you know that you're free. Free to become whoever you are. Free to create a life that's true for you. Whatever shape that takes, we'll be cheering you on.

To the congregation I once served: Thank you. Literally everyone who came to and *through* EastLake. For the trust, the questions, the heartbreak, and the beauty. You shaped me, and I carry both the wounds and the wisdom with me still. So much gratitude.

To the INCREDIBLE staff team I served with during my years at the church: Thank you for your courage, your grit, your creativity, and your heart. We carried so much together. And we laughed a lot too. For all the pressure and unpredictability, there was so much joy in what we built, so many good-hearted people doing meaningful work, making room for others, and somehow still making a point to have a fucking blast and celebrate life. I'll always be grateful for your trust, your talent, your humor, and the ways we stretched and struggled and sometimes thrived as we tried to build something that mattered. Thank you for seeing me when I didn't know who I was and loving me anyway. This book is stitched together with your grace. Know that whenever something good happens in your life, my heart swells.

Special thanks to the OG staffers who went the distance: **Amy Olason, Sarah Nienaber, Heather Lewis, and Darin Hansen** for being a part of more change than most people see in a lifetime. You saw it all. You *were* EastLake.

"Undying, groveling on my knees before you" thanks to the intrepid leadership team of **Kristen Burchinal and Peter Gadd**: You held me together. You carried more stress than anyone should've had to. You stayed steady when everything around us shook. And you graciously helped me make the hardest decision of all; leaving. I won't forget that.

To Aaron Noble: for over a decade of showing up, carrying weight I didn't always see, and supporting me in more ways than I'll ever fully know. I'm glad you were my assistant for all those years just so that we could enjoy what emerged in loving friendship after the roles were done. You are family.

To Leah Harris: For always loving me as Ryan from day one. For never needing me to be anything other than myself. And for doing so much LSD with me. You are an angel. I love you.

To Pat McJunkin: My friend since we were thirteen, thank you for believing in this crazy church and starting it with us. And thank you most of all for showing up for the most Important *fuck you* moment of my life. I needed that. You knew it, and you didn't hesitate. That meant more than I can say.

To David Lunsford: For one of the greatest seasons of friendship in my life. For the road trips, your beautiful, honest music, and the depth and laughter you brought to everything. You were the homie I couldn't have made it without.

To Eric Nienaber: for being the best brother-in-law I could ask for, and for everything you gave from the very beginning. Thank you for trusting me with your precious sister. We both love you so much.

To Tyson Chester: What a gift to have had a friend on the outside of all that religious shit who never cared either way. Thanks for coming to

Africa with me. For sharing all the festivals, the VWs and the adventures. Thanks for truly seeing our kids. You and Rachael are chosen family.

To Grant Enloe, Tom Noble, Jason Lewis, and Jonah McKee: For all the laughter, the brotherhood, and the Boardman trips. For believing in me when it was hard, and for being the kind of friends I could count on to tell me what I needed to hear. The truth.

To Dave Nelson, Jeremy Johnson, Ryan Farmer, and Matt Woll: For being my men-at-arms during those wild seasons of growth, when we were basically building the airplane in midair. And to **George Mekhail**, for sticking with it when it wasn't as cool and sexy anymore. For holding the line to preserve our team as long as possible. And for reminding me: no regrets when we're 90.

To Andy Burchinal: For being a solid friend who was always down to kick anyone's ass if I needed it. And for building some of the most important physical spaces that held my heart when it was tough. Your loyalty showed up in wood and nails, and I felt it.

To Katie Haynes: For having the absolute sharpest sense of humor. You kill me. For laughing way too loud during sermon filming days. For loving me through so much of my reintegration.

To Jessica and Stephen Rose: Thanks for sliding down the slope at the same time so that we had someone to talk to on the way down. And for visiting us so much. We feel so loved.

To Ben and Amanda Langhans: For being real ones. For your tenacious pursuit of personal growth. And for believing in me on both sides of the journey. You guys inspire me.

To Warren McCaig: For finding me when you did, bringing Michelle and I to Bolivia, and expanding our scope of possibility. And for hyping me up when this book started leaking out of me at your house. The future is ours, dude!

To the mentors and guides who helped me along the way:

- **Bruce Sanguin**: For giving me something new to believe in. For ushering me into altered states that helped make me a better human.

- **Kent Dobson**: Meeting you at just the right time put wind in my sails and a smile back on my face. Thanks for being a true friend and for so many special memories in the woods. That season we got to share was one of my favorites. Thanks for always being you. Getting you laughing is still one of my favorite things.

- **Peter Rollins**: For being a safe place when I didn't know who I was or where I was going. For letting me be in process and meeting me as a human. I've learned so much from your incredible mind, but the most enduring thing is your deep kindness.

- **Rick Enloe**: The realest of the real. You were a true north star. Thank you for loving me like you did. I miss you.

- **Brian McLaren** and **Doug Pagitt**: For the fatherly way you showed up when I needed steadiness, perspective, and heart.

- **Rob Bell**: For the surf chats, the crucial phone calls, and for flying up on your own dime to encourage our staff when we were taking a ton of heat. That was amazing.

- **Bill Berger**: for showing up that Saturday in 2015 and telling me I was still loved.

To Justin Jaquith: for reaching out and offering to edit this mess of a book and helping me shape it into something coherent. You believed in me and this message. That meant so much.

To the Encinitas soul cluster, Adam, Jonas, Gilly, Thai Ha, Summer, Kat, Taryn, and Taylor: You met us in this world in a way that was so pure and so healing. Thank you for loving us just for being us. For the cuddle puddles, the adventures, the barefoot beach days, and the wild, ordinary magic of being together. What a time.

To my in-laws: Thank you for raising the most incredible human being I've ever known. Michelle is the greatest miracle in my life. Thank you for letting me marry her way too early. For treating me like a son since I was a teenager. You make me feel so loved.

To my parents: Thank you for your love, your prayers, and your willingness to keep walking with me, even when the road changed. I know my path hasn't always been easy to understand, but you've never stopped showing up with kindness, with care, and with grace. Thank you for trusting that I'm still your son, even as I've changed. You embody Jesus in a beautiful way, and I respect that so much. I see your faith, I see your hearts, and I see the ways you've continued to choose love over fear. That means more than I can say.

Finally, to everyone who cheered me on, challenged me, carried me, or cautioned me about the slippery slope: Thanks for the push.

ABOUT THE AUTHOR

From ordained ministry to psychedelic chaplaincy, Ryan Meeks has spent his life exploring what it means to be fully human.

For decades, he and his wife, Michelle, led one of the first evangelical mega-churches in the U.S. to fully affirm and include the LGBTQ+ community. But after surviving cancer and dismantling his own belief system, Ryan turned his focus to helping others navigate transformation. He now helps people who've lost their religion but not their longing rewrite the script—turning deconstruction into embodied love, brave partnership, and a life that actually works.

In their day-to-day practice, Ryan and Michelle facilitate retreats, lead transformational couples work, provide (un)spiritual direction and integration coaching, and offer personalized fitness and nutrition guidance. Their mission is to help people feel alive, find deeper meaning, and cultivate relationships grounded in love and presence.

They live in Encinitas, California, with their two youngest sons.

Ryan still sucks at surfing.

www.ingramcontent.com/pod-product-compliance
Lightning Source LLC
Chambersburg PA
CBHW071319090426
42738CB00012B/2737